THE BLUEPRINT FOR HEARING GOD

Your One-Stop Guide to Intuitive Listening and Operation

Jason H. Jackson

(The Blueprint For Hearing GOD)
Copyright © 2020 by (Dr. Jason H. Jackson)

All rights reserved. No part of this book may be reproduced or transmitted in any form or by any means without written permission from the author.

Unless otherwise indicated, all Scripture quotations are taken from the Holy Bible, New International Version®, NIV®, © 1973, 1978, 1984 by the International Bible Society. Scripture quotations taken from the Amplified® Bible (AMPC), © 1954, 1958, 1962, 1964, 1965, 1987 by The Lockman Foundation Used by permission. All rights reserved. Scripture quotations marked (NKJV) are taken from the New King James Version, © 1979, 1980, 1982, 1984 by Thomas Nelson, Inc. Used by permission. Scripture quotations marked (KJV) are taken from the King James Version of the Holy Bible. Scripture quotations marked (NASB) are taken from the updated New American Standard Bible®, NASB ®, © 1960, 1962, 1963, 1968, 1971, 1972, 1973, 1975, 1977, 1995 by The Lockman Foundation. Used by permission (www.Lockman.org). Some definitions of Hebrew and Greek words are taken from Strong's Exhaustive Concordance, Vine's Complete Expository Dictionary of Old and New Testament Word. Some dictionary definitions are taken from Merriam-Webster's 11th Collegiate Dictionary.

Paperback ISBN 13:978-0-9965867-3-3

Table of Contents

Preface: **Satisfying The World's Groan For Identity** vii

Chapter 1: **The World's Demand for Dimensionally Intuitive People**   1
Establishing the Definition and Purpose
of Human Instinct   1

Section 1: Entering the Gates   2

Answering "The Call" to Make Calls   2
Harmonizing With the Language of Science   4
Defining the Dimensionally Intuitive Person   5

Chapter 2: **The Mechanics of Human Intuitiveness**   7
Unlocking Human Composition and Construct   7

Section 1: Discovering Human Composition and Construction   8
Defining Your Natural and Intuitive Nature   8

Section 2: The Human Soul and Body   11
Your Greatest Opponents to Intuitive Operation   11
The Purpose and Beauty of a Human's Soul   12

Section 3: The Function of The Human Spirit   15

Your Immortal Identity & Transdimensional Vehicle   15
The Human Spirit Our Hidden Identity   15
The Human Spirit's Partnership With The Holy Spirit   17
11 Common Debates Between Your Soul and Spirit   18

Chapter 3: **Establishing Your Intuitive Purpose**   21
Activating Personal Authority &
Domain Through Intuitive Listening   21

Section 1: The Law of Intuitive-Based

Organizational Management — 22
The Reason Why We Must Hear from GOD — 22
Character-Based Management >
Talents and Intuitive Abilities — 25

Section 2: Intrinsic Personal Authority — 27
Your Authorization to Manage Your Domain — 27
3 Steps to Activating Personal-authority — 28

Chapter 4: **Partnering With The Premier Intuitive Guide** — 33
Dimensions and Operations of The Holy Spirit — 33

Section 1: Your Most Valuable Relationship — 34
The Holy Spirit, Your Guide to Intuitive Listening — 34
32 Operations of The Holy Spirit — 35
4 Dimensions of Relationship with The Holy Spirit — 37
The Third-Dimension of Relationship With The Holy Spirit — 39
Shifting from the First to Second-Dimension of Relationship With The Holy Spirit — 40
Shifting from the Second to Third-Dimension of Relationship With The Holy Spirit — 41

Section 2: The Framework for Intuitive Listening — 43
Decoding Intuitive Prompts From The Holy Spirit — 43
The 6 Major Intuitive Prompts From The Holy Spirit — 44

Chapter 5: **Releasing Dormant Intuitive Abilities** — 48
Opening, Managing and Deploying Spiritual Gifts — 48

Section 1: Reinstating Intuitive Function — 49
A Child's Story of Unopened Gifts — 49
4 Principles of Managing Your Wealth of Gifts — 50
Balancing the Terms Spiritual, Intuitive, Supernatural and Metaphysical — 53

Section 2: The Purpose of Intuitive Gifts — 55

Becoming an Ambassador of Heaven — 55
7 Assignments For Intuitive Communicators — 56

Chapter 6: **Understanding Intuitive Dimensions of Operation** — 60
Clarifying Spiritual Streams and Functions — 60

Section 1: Tools of Intuitive Operation — 61
*Influencing What You Have Heard
With What You Have* — 61
*Streams and Functions of 21 Common
Supernatural Gifts* — 62

Chapter 7: **Discerning The Revelatory Dimension** — 73
Identifying the Source of Intuitive Messages — 73

Section 1: The Destination of Intuitive Messages — 74
Navigating the Voices in Our Minds — 74
Your Soul, Gatekeeper of Intuitive Messages — 74

Section 2: Navigating the Realm of Intuitive Messages — 78
Identifying 4 Sources of Intuitive Messages — 78
Managing the 4 Sources of Intuitive Messages — 85

Section 3: Subconscious Intuitive Intervention — 87
Embracing Dreams as Intuitive Messages — 87

Chapter 8: **Decoding The Revelatory Dimension** — 90
Interpreting Advanced Intuitive Messages — 90

Section 1: The Source and Purpose of Prophetic Messages — 91
The Source of Prophetic Interpretation — 91
Interpreting the 5 Purposes of Prophetic Messages — 92
Identifying 5 Structures of Prophetic Messages — 95

Section 3: Interpreting Symbolism in

Prophetic Messages — 98
Interpreting 6 Common Symbols Found in Prophetic Messages — 98

Section 4: Interpreting the Proper Application of Prophetic Messages — 102
Identifying the 4 Points of Application in Prophetic Messages — 102

Section 5: Deploying Safeguards for Prophetic Interpretation — 105
Outlining the Five Steps of Prophetic Interpretation — 105
Deploying the Five Steps of Prophetic Interpretation — 105

Chapter 9: Releasing The Revelatory Dimension — 110
Safeguarding and Delivering Prophetic Messages — 110

Section 1: Delivering Prophetic Messages — 111
Leveraging the Dimension of Faith — 111
Six Stages of Managing Effective Prophetic Message Delivery — 112

Section 2: 10 Intuitive Channels — 116
Specified Content for Prophetic Messages — 116

Final Section: Closing Remarks — 122

About the Author — 124

Appendix 'A': Quick Reference Guides — 127

Appendix 'B': Glossary of Common Signs and Symbols — 133

Preface

Satisfying the World's Groan For Identity

As the world exited the 20th century, life as we once knew it all but vanished. The many nomenclatures used to define our moral basis, political affiliation, career aspirations, and various life positions ended with an era. What is the point of a definition? Are definitions necessary? Specified definitions demonstrate that a legitimate "thought process" was assigned in characterizing the purpose of individual jobs, groups, objects, and spirituality. Through crafted definitions, we can assign appropriate values.

How do we define the responsibility of roles? Today's intense political climate is, at times, piloted by those who render policy decisions by popular demand instead of factual data. Rather than welfare accountability, social acceptance tends to drive the message of today's spiritual leaders. Parents have abandoned their families for self-pursual. Grandparents forgo retirement to support capable adult children. How did we arrive at such social disarray?

Our definitions set a precedent for our expectations. We are failing at defining personal identities and corresponding responsibilities in life's multitude of roles. When individuals inadequately identify themselves, they enter into the world's social, economic, and political structures. This causes malfunctions throughout global communities. To be most effective at our roles, we must first journey to identify and define our in- dividual attributes and unique abilities.

The advent of the information era allowed humanity instant access to an abundance of data, absent the maturity-causing processes formerly required to attain it. The aforementioned has resulted in many embracing identities based on constant social exposure, rather than intuitive, self-exploration. Through good-old-fashioned introspection, humanity can discover fingerprints defining their naturally-supernatural identity and extraordinary ability to achieve greatness in all life's aspects.

Chapter 1

The World's Demand for Dimensionally Intuitive People

Establishing the Definition and Purpose of Human Instinct

Entering the Gates

Answering "The Call" to Make Calls

Should hunger be present in any stretch of the globe? What could prevent a nation from experiencing economic collapse? What should a person do to find true happiness? Through ordinary means, the world's best and brightest have strained to answer such questions. Humanity has enhanced agriculture to feed the hungry, developed technology to balance financial markets and advanced medicine to heal broken hearts. Still, we struggle to provide answers and solutions to the world's most complex problems.

Fortunately, some are willing to dedicate their intuitive abilities to solving these complex issues. The exceptional aptitude of mature, intuitive people allows them to draw upon the unseen, distinguishing the difference from the way things are and the way they were initially designed. Who are these seemingly extraordinary people? One could liken intuitive people to engineers. For every engineer, there is a blueprint.

Engineers have a unique ability to analyse a blueprint and pinpointing the intentions of the architect. Similarly, through their intuitive gifts, "Life Engineers" help to identify the framework set by the "Master Architect" known as GOD, the Creator of all things.

Commonly called "prophetic" or "intuitive" people, GOD has used Life Engineers for millennia. They derive from all ethnic, social, and professional backgrounds, and use their intuitive ability to reinstate GOD's original purpose for individuals and the world's communities.

The world is evolving at an immeasurable pace. Unlike the survival-focus of those living in, modern day people spend countless hours scouring the internet, watching videos, and messaging. The introduction of the internet hurdled most geographical limitations. Through automation, many time-consuming tasks requiring the collection and distribution of data are completed in mere seconds. Ultimately, these advances need humanity to exercise profound levels of responsibility.

The human race must determine whether technological innovations produce positive or harmful impacts on our communities. **When humankind acquires new power, it is always best served when guided by moral influence, the best of which comes from GOD and is often delivered by HIS intuitive people.**

Where are the people who can unravel the miscalculations of Wall Street, while speaking words of comfort and guidance to those suffering from subjugation? Where are those with the transcendent vision to identify future food, power, and water shortages while providing a means to prevent such catastrophes?

The same framework which established the obstacles is investigating them. I have often said that **it is nearly impossible to solve problems on the same level of their creation.** With nominal effort, college seniors capably tutor elementary students. Their engagement requires descending into a realm of thought they have once visited. Similarly, intuitive people can step in and out of places that GOD has once visited, descending with information to support those who are in need.

On January 27, 1986, John Paul Jackson, a well-known Christian prophetic voice, called NASA with a severe warning regarding his intuitive vision of the space shuttle Challenger exploding. Regrettably, the team could not accept or possibly even believe his message. On January 28, 1986, seventy-three seconds into its flight, the Challenger exploded tragically, taking all lives on board. John Paul Jackson saw the unseen, and although it could have cost him his credibility, he made the call. If both answered and received, that call could have saved lives. Maybe you can make the call that protects your family, community, or even your country. Are you prepared to answer the call of making calls? Are you ready to hear and see the mind of GOD?

Harmonizing With the Language of Science

At this point, you must be wondering why I am using pseudo-biblical-psychological and scientifically inspired words. My answer is straightforward. **People reject the things that they do not have the capacity to receive or comprehend.** Conversely, as you will learn in the proceeding chapters, a significant key to delivering an intuitive message is that: **In life, you can choose to get your point across or accomplish an objective. The two do not necessarily correlate. Be objective orientated.** This book is intended to strengthen the foundation of those who believe in the supernatural abilities and purpose promised, and given by Jesus Christ. Secondarily, I hope to encourage those who are scientifically critical, off the fence of partiality.

For over 20 years, I have been an adamant supporter, student, and admirer of the sciences. Correspondingly, I have come to the personal conclusion that **science helps us to explain the created world, but cannot explain the One who created it.** Science is rendered powerless when attempting to examine "Someone" who pre-exists the very time and space which governs its calculations.

Though I continue to consider myself a scientist at heart, I must express my belief that the Judeo-Christian Bible is infallible. Nevertheless, science often helps us to articulate the world around us in language that is more palatable to the average person. As a seasoned entrepreneur who also serves as a spiritual leader, I understand traditional Christian words of expression often serve as a barrier to those seeking the truth.

Throughout my travels, I have found that Christian teachers often favour words that encourage tradition over words that promote comprehension. Today, an emphasis must be placed on being objective orientated. **It is better to be understood than heard.** Besides, Jesus said that He came for the recon- ciliation of the sick, hurting, and those who did not know GOD. We should assume they were people who may not have spoken the "temple language." Jesus was the master at bringing others to an awareness of His Father through words balanced by easy comprehension, potency, and cultural relevancy. Hopefully, this book will follow in His wake.

Defining the Dimensionally Intuitive Person

The world desires intuitive people who can inspire its conduct and direction. History reminds us that when non-intuitive people manage the world, a form of calamity or implosion follows. Three dimensional, ordinary people are controlled by their knowledge, solely based on experiential statistics. Their past often serves in dictation to their future, reintroducing my statement: We will always struggle in our attempt to solve problems on the same level by which they were created.

Contrastingly, dimensionally intuitive people often excel in areas where they possess little to no familiarity. The word *intuitive* describes the ability to acquire knowledge absent physical inspirations, i.e., taking classes or having a prior understanding. For the purposed of this book, the word "dimensional" refers to the function of operating in multiple realms and planes of existence, beyond the naturally seen, three-dimensional world. Consequently, **a dimensionally intuitive person can acquire knowledge from varying planes of existence without the need of prior physical experience.**

Have you always believed there is more available to you than the eye can see? Have you experienced success in life, but still feel incomplete? Looking back at your life, would you say that others come to you seeking your advice and wisdom? If you have answered yes to these questions, you have come to the right place. I believe this book was inspired by GOD to unlock the greatness that dwells within you. Please pay close attention and hold on for the ride because we have much ground to cover.

What to Take Away From This Chapter

You should now know that there is a demand for dimensionally intuitive people.

Hopefully, this section has inspired you to learn more about who you are.

Key Points From Chapter 1

1. People reject the things they do not have the capacity to receive or comprehend. If you wish to deliver powerful, intuitive messages, you must use self-control and tact. Focus on objectives rather than getting the point across, and you will be understood, instead of simply heard.
2. Commonly called "prophetic" or "intuitive" people, Life Engineers have been used by GOD for millennia, deriving from all ethnics, social, and professional backgrounds. Strategically placed, they used their intuitive ability to reinstate GOD's original purpose for individuals and the world's communities.
3. When humankind is endowed with new power, it is always best served when guided by moral influence, the best of which comes from GOD and is often delivered by HIS intuitive people.
4. It is nearly impossible to solve problems on the same level in which they were created.
5. People reject the things they do not have the capacity to receive or comprehend. If you wish to deliver powerful, intuitive messages, you must use self-control and tact. Focus on objectives rather than getting the point across, and you will be understood, instead heard.
6. Science helps us to explain the created world, but cannot explain the One who created it. Science is rendered powerless when attempting to examine "Someone" who pre-exists the very time and space which governs its calculations.

Chapter 2

The Mechanics of Human Intuitiveness

Unlocking Human Composition and Construct

Section1: Discovering Human Composition and Construction

Defining Your Natural and Intuitive Nature

To establish a solid framework in intuitive operation, you must first be clear about your true identity and capabilities. Accordingly, I welcome you with this statement. **You are a Spirit with a body, not a body with a Spirit. You're a Spiritual-being experiencing Earth.** In most major religions, the totality of being "Human" is divided into three parts; Soul, Spirit, and Body. Judeo-Christian understandings equate the Soul to the recognizable functions of the human brain, working in conjunction with an immortal human Spirit with both residing in a physical structure called a body.

Consider your television for a moment. Before receiving input from an invisible Wi-Fi connection, the screen is blank or still. Once a connection is made, images are projected to your screen from a server in a distant, unseen location. The Soul receives hidden information from your Spirit as television gets data from a Wi-Fi signal. As a Spiritual Being, you have access to dimensions far more significant than the apparent three-dimensional world in which we occupy. **True human intuition exists through your Spirit, outside of the constraints of time and space, and is not restricted to the Body or Soul.**

As a Spirit-being, you can be anywhere at any time.

Scientifically speaking, the Spiritual aspect of your being is non-local in the same sense that quantum objects are non-local. Quantum physicists assert the human brain is a super-computer processing the informational state of micro-mechanics (qubits) remitted by your multidimensional Spirit. Though locked in the physical world, the Soul is receiving undetected information (from the future and unknown present) gathered from the Spirit daily. If you've ever experienced "déjà vu," also known as "precognition," this explanation may offer solace.

Philosophers and scientists have debated for millennia on exactly how this process functions from a mechanical viewpoint. I am sure the debate will continue.

Biblically, although some translations use the terms Soul and Spirit interchangeably, through scripture, they are entirely different. To function effectively as an intuitive person, you must never get the two confused. **The Hebrew word for Soul is "Nefesh," with Spirit translating to the Hebrew for "Neshma."** Conversely, this is a crucial point reflecting the words for Soul and Spirit were not intended to be interchangeable. An improper definition will lead to misdiagnosis of the origins and purpose of humans. **By lacking comprehension of human composition, we search for eternal answers through a finite lens.**

In the scripture below, Paul delivers a clear distinction between the Soul and the Spirit, suggesting that each has their own set of ideas. However, Jesus, also known as "The Word of GOD," has the capacity to differentiate between them so you can understand and operate within your highest ability.

> "For the word of God is living and active, sharper than any two-edged sword, piercing to the division of <u>soul and of spirit</u>, of joints and marrow, and discerning the thoughts and intentions of the heart."-Paul of Tarsus, Letter to the Hebrews 4:12

Intuitive listening requires that you see and hear prompts from outside of our three-dimensional world. This function involves communication from your Spirit to your Soul. As you continue to gain a clearer picture of your composition, you will find you are naturally supernatural, specially designed to be intuitive. For those attempting to hear from GOD, I am sure that your focal concern is whether you are hearing your voice or the words of GOD. For this reason, I must take time over the next two sections to help you conclude the differences between your Soul and your Human Spirit.

What to Take Away From This Section

You should now understand that you are a triune being engineered to function beyond the five senses.

Key Points From Section 1

1. You are a Spirit with a body, not a body with a Spirit. You're a Spiritual Being living an earthly experience through a three-dimensional body.
2. The totality of a Human Being is divided into three parts; Soul, Spirit, and Body.
3. The Soul receives unseen information from your Spirit as television gets data from a Wi-Fi signal. As a Spiritual Being, you have access to dimensions far more significant than the apparent three-dimensional world in which we occupy.
4. True human intuition exists through your Spirit, outside of the constraints of time and space, and is not restricted to the Body or Soul.
5. The Hebrew word for Soul is "Nefesh," with Spirit translating to the Hebrew for "Neshma." The words for Soul and Spirit we not intended to be interchangeable.
6. Those who do not comprehend the composition of man search for eternal answers through a finite lens. By lacking comprehension of human composition, we search for eternal answers through a finite lens.
7. Intuitive listening requires that you see and hear prompts from outside of our three-dimensional world. This function involves communication from your Spirit to your Soul.

Section 2: The Human Soul and Body

Your Greatest Opponents to Intuitive Operation

In the 8th-century poem, Beowulf introduced the term "Soul" to the English language. At a glance, this poem appears to have encouraged generations of tying the words "Soul" and "Spirit" as one, interchangeable unit. There are impeccable distinctions between a human's mortal Soul and immortal Spirit.

The Soul is the combination of faculties consisting of the "Mind," "Will," "Emotions," and "Intellect," among others. Adam, the first human, was created from the dust of the Earth and became a living Soul. Because of this, our natural senses, contained within our Souls, are attuned to the Earth, and our feelings often shift and align according to what is happening around us. In contrast to your Spirit, your Soul performs the emotional, rational, and intellectual functions required for you to respond within this three-dimensional world.

Humans share the Soul in common with other animals. In the absence of our Spirit, we are much like most mammals. For instance, your dog has a Soul. He hungers (Mind), makes decisions (Will), desires affection (Emotions), knows when he has done wrong, and can complete complex tasks (Intellect). These are all essential functions encompassed by the realm of the Soul.

Spiritual or intuitive operation, however, is reserved only through the human's Spirit.

Ordinary people typically choose inspiration conceived by their limited, three-dimensionally-focused Soul. If a dog is bitten, usually his instinct leads him to return the bite immediately. When an "ordinary" (Soul-focused by choice) person is provoked, they will likely respond in like manner. If humankind has the option of living in superior magnitudes through the vehicle of their Spirit, why do we often choose the same vessel (Soul) as a four-legged animal?

Humans are naturally supernatural. Ordinary people are only ordinary by choice. It is their continued choice of the Soul as their life's governor, which makes them ordinary.

What if your destiny is to be the first in your family to start a business? What if you lacked the experience and financial resources to start the business? Would you still believe in the possibility of entrepreneurship? Your intellect, mind, and emotions will likely serve as deterrence by emphasizing the deficit of your past and present. Consider this: Some of the greatest minds of the world, such as Bill Gates, did not complete college or had any rational motive to build Microsoft.

As a GOD-inspired, intuitive person, HE will invite you to areas you never dreamed of, as HE did with so many others as recorded by the Bible. Though when HE speaks, you cannot allow your Soul to govern your reply. Here is a thought, **GOD will not take a supernatural idea and deposit it into the natural mind of the Soul**. I will further elaborate on this topic in Section 4.

The Purpose and Beauty of a Human's Soul

Although mature, intuitive people are primarily guided by their Spirit, the Soul plays crucial role in human life. **The Soul possesses distinct purposes such as aiding earthly connectivity, human community, and free will.** The majority of the seen universe comprises of non-thinking, unconscious, "inanimate" objects. The sun burns, stars twinkle, and the ocean returns to its place without thought. Have you noticed– even though they are inanimate- how much they inspire your Soul when you need it most?

A walk on the beach under the glaze of the sun can quickly bring our mind and emotions into balance. We stand in awe while gazing at the stars and moon. Why? Initially, you learned that from dust, our Souls and Bodies were designed to tie us to the world around us. The sun, moon, and Earth were all created for bringing connectivity to your Soul during your stay in this three-dimensional world.

Your Soul also serves in supporting human community. In my definition, **community is the social structure that nourishes and advances the lives of those within it.** Imagine if you cried while surrounded by laughing onlookers. Unfortunately, this emotional disconnect occurs daily throughout humanity. Contrastingly, consider the many moments when your friends both laughed and cried with you during your highest and lowest moments. For many of us, it is these moments that give us the WILL (a function of the Soul) to remain hopeful. "Governed by the manufacturer, GOD, human communities thrive through renewed Souls exhibiting properly kindled emotions, balanced minds, and selfless exchange of intellect."

Your Soul is the free-will mediator between your Body and your Spirit and is constantly being dragged in either direction. Your body focuses on its desire to protect and preserve itself while your Spirit fixates on the supernatural. The body wants to eat and exercise, but the Spirit wants to operate in supernatural realms. For some, the Spirit is drawn to prayer while Body wants to sleep. The battle of all battles. The victor over your Soul will ultimately determine the course of your life.

However, make no mistake, **your construction was designed, in part, to foster your ability to choose GOD from the confines of your three dimensional Body.** There is much more to share about this topic. For now, please acknowledge that **there is a silent battle intended to constrain you to the finite dimensions of your Soul and Body.** I hope you will personally declare to day by day, fight to win the war from within, and live according to your original design.

What to Take Away From This Section

You should now understand that the human Soul comprises basic animal functions that were derived from the Earth. We should appreciate the aspects of the Soul and focus on the development of its characteristics.

Key Points From Section 2

1. The Soul is the combination of faculties consisting of the "Mind," "Will," "Emotions" and "Intellect," among others.
2. Many animals, such as dogs, possess a Soul. They hunger (Mind), makes decisions (Will), desire affection (Emotions), know when they have done wrong, and can complete complex tasks (Intellect).
3. Humans are naturally supernatural. Ordinary people are only ordinary by choice. It is their continued choice of the Soul as their life's governor, which makes them ordinary. GOD will not take a supernatural idea and deposit it into the natural mind of the Soul.
4. The Soul possesses distinct purposes, such as aiding earthly connectivity, human community, and free-will.
5. Community is the social structure that nourishes and advances the lives of those within it.
6. Governed by the manufacturer, GOD, human communities thrive through renewed Souls exhibiting properly kindled emotions, balanced minds, and selfless exchanges of intellect.
7. Your Soul is the free-will mediator between your body and your Spirit; it can be dragged in either direction. This construction was designed, in part, to foster your ability to choose GOD from the confines of your three-dimensional body.
8. There is a silent battle intended to constrain you to the finite dimensions of your Soul and Body.

Section 3: The Function of The Human Spirit

Your Immortal Identity & Transdimensional Vehicle

The term *immortal* refers to having an exemption from death. The word *transdimensional* suggests the prospect of multidimensional (spiritual) functionality and operation. After reading the first two sections, you should be clear that your Soul and Body were primarily engineered to cover the three-dimensional aspects of life. Now let us begin with the understanding that in contrast to your Soul and Body, your Human Spirit is immortal and transdimensional.

Non-local, your Human Spirit gives you the ability to transcend dimensions such as space, time, and other unknown dimensions. To many, the mere idea of extraordinary, super-human ability brings about excitement. However, our excitement should not be surrounded by newness, but self-discovery of originality. As a Spirit, you are metaphysical in nature. The word, metaphysical, is derived from the term *meta ta physika, which* refers to the idea that there is a functional reality outside of the perception of our Soul and Body.

Mostly, the terms "spiritual" and "metaphysical" are interchangeable. As mentioned, **you are a Spirit with a Body, not a Body with a Spirit. You are a spiritual being living the human experience through the eyes of a human body.** I empathize with this being an involved principal to embrace. However, your depth comprehension regarding your true spiritual identity will act as a gauge for your functioning within your intuitive abilities on Earth.

The Human Spirit Our Hidden Identity

From conception, GOD engrafts our Human Body, Soul, and Spirit together. **Within the confines of our Spirits, we can uncover everything that GOD intended for our lives to flourish within human form on Earth.** As mentioned at the beginning of the chapter, although I fancy both scientific and novelty terminologies, I support the authenticity of the Judeo-Christian Bible. My conviction is that when we read the Bible through intuitive eyes, we discover its multidimensional expression.

For those still critical, the Judeo-Christian Bible contains nearly "300" prophetic passages that describe Jesus in great detail. Among all, there are "60 "major predictions. The likelihood of the Bible predicting Jesus' fulfilment of just "8" prophecies is equal to 1 x 1028 or 1 in 10,000,000,000,000,000,000,000,000,000. Statically speaking, your chance of becoming president is estimated to be equal to 1 x 107 or 1 in 10,000,000. While you consider the numbers, know there is more to the Bible than what meets the natural eye.

Are we Bodies with Spirits or Spirits with Bodies? Assuming that you accept my prior statement, let's look to the Bible for a moment. According to Genesis 1:27, GOD said, "Let us *create* man in our image and in our likeness." As you will identify shortly, in this declaration, GOD was referring to the human Spirit being established in HIS image and in HIS likeness. Why does this matter?

If the statement is true, then you are in the very image of GOD HIMSELF! With this, it would make perfect sense that your true identity is both immortal and multidimensional. **If you are confused about GOD's image, you will also be con- fused about your image**. In just one verse before, in Genesis 1:26, the Bible says, "GOD *made* man in HIS image and likeness." **The word "make" refers to the act of com- posing something out of existing materials. The word "create" equates to bringing something into existence.** Had the sequence been in the natural order, GOD would have created man first, then made the functions of man. Since when do we *make* something before *creat*ing it?

The word Spirit is derived from the Greek word "pneuma," which translates to breath. After GOD "made" the structure of your human Body and Soul

out of the Earth's ground, HE blew HIS breath into your animal frame, calling your immortal Spirit to engraft into it for residence in this three-dimensional world. GOD is an eternal Spirit. Therefore, in John's 3rd chapter of the Judeo-Christian Bible, he wrote, "Flesh bears flesh and spirit bears spirit," it means that GOD bore an eternal human Spirit (You) in HIS likeness.

As a Spirit being, you were created by GOD to be multidimensional and supernatural. As a Spirit, you are purposed to communicate with Eternity HIMSELF. I must reiterate, **you are a Spirit with a Body and Soul, not a Body and Soul with Spirit. Your Spirit is the epitome of who you are. Your Spirit establishes you as an immortal, multidimensional, and multifaceted being, just as GOD, in HIS image.** Why then, do we not choose to operate as supernatural beings more frequently?

The Human Spirit's Partnership With The Holy Spirit

The previous section elaborated on the purpose of the Soul as a vehicle for earthly connection and human community. I also mentioned that the Soul must be governed by GOD to function according to its original design. Now understand that GOD governs your Soul in collaboration with your Spirit. **The Supernatural GOD only partners with the supernatural aspect of humans.**

Ultimately, if we want to partner with GOD, we must move beyond the known and into hidden places only known to our Spirit. Like us, GOD is a three-part being: Spirit (GOD the Creator), Body (Jesus), and Soul (The Holy Spirit). GOD partners with us through the Holy Spirit. In Paul's 8th letter to the Romans of the Judeo-Christian Bible he said, **The Spirit himself bears witness with our spirit that we are children of GOD.** Here, Paul clarifies that GOD speaks to and through our human Spirit, not our Soul.

11 Common Debates Between Your Soul and Spirit

To reiterate, when your Spirit is enlightened by the Holy Spirit, through salvation, the will of GOD is made known to your Spirit. Notice I expressed, "the will of GOD is made known to you." This means that you can know the *Mind of GOD*, not just for yourself but for others. The catch is, however, your Spirit has to convince your Soul that the other- worldly communication received from the Holy Spirit is real. Typically, this will yield a daily challenge.

By design, GOD breathed you out of eternity (HIMSELF) and into your body so you would have a fair opportunity to choose HIM in a semi-blind state. If you are to partner with GOD, you must differentiate between the voices of your Soul and Spirit. The chart below offers 11 typical debates between your Soul and Spirit.

Common Suggestions From Your Soul
1. This situation is hopeless.
2. I blew it last time, it won't work now.
3. People do not notice you because you're_____.
4. No one cares about you.
5. You are all alone and will always be.
6. Give up!
7. It's too late to fix it.
8. Nothing I can do will help.
9. I am not important to GOD.
10. GOD is mad at me because_____.
11. Everyone else gets good things, but not you.

Common Responses From Your Spirit

1. This situation will change.
2. You've learned since the last time.
3. You're crafted in the image of GOD stay true, and others will see.
4. GOD established people in your life to love you.
5. Jesus is with you and will always be.
6. Keep going!
7. It's never too late to fix it.
8. GOD can and will help.
9. GOD hasn't forgotten you.
10. GOD knew you would do _____ before you did.
11. You also have received good things, and your time is near for more, be patient.

What to Take Away From This Section

You should now understand that you are a triune being engineered to work with a triune GOD. You now know that your Spirit becomes perfected when it comes into union with the Holy Spirit, through GOD'S gift of salvation through Jesus.

Key Points From Section 3

1. You are a Spirit with a Body, not a Body with a Spirit. You are a spiritual being living the human experience through the eyes of a human body.
2. Within the confines of our Spirit, we can uncover everything that GOD intended for our lives to flourish while in human form on Earth.
3. GOD established you supernaturally by making you first (your Body and Soul) and creating you second, pulling your Spirit out of Himself and engrafting you to your Body and Soul. Just as GOD, your true identity is both immortal and multidimensional. If you are confused about GOD's image, you will also be confused about your image.
4. The Supernatural GOD only partners with the supernatural aspect of Humans. To partner with GOD, we must move beyond the known and into hidden places only known to our Spirit, by faith.
5. When salvation occurs (accepting Jesus as your Lord and Savior), your Spirit is enlightened by the Holy Spirit. When the will of GOD is made known to your Spirit, you can know the "Mind of GOD" for your life and the life of others.
6. Your Spirit has the challenge of convincing your Soul that the otherworldly communication received from the Holy Spirit is real.

Chapter 3

Establishing Your Intuitive Purpose

Activating Personal Authority & Domain Through Intuitive Listening

Section 1: The Law of Intuitive-Based Organizational Management

The Reason Why We Must Hear from GOD

People who actively hear GOD understand that HE often communicates regarding the management of HIS resources. HE speaks concerning their current handling and how they should be managed to accomplish HIS will. Please understand, **GOD speaks with intention and purpose. If you evolve into a person of intention and purpose, HE will speak with you more frequently.**

The other day I watched my mother digging around in her garden as she admired the beauty of her tomatoes and kale. Though I have always appreciated gardens, I never considered the continuous "management" required to maintain them. As I continued to ponder this idea, I realized that **the primary difference between a jungle and a garden is organizational management.** The beautiful jungle can wildly grow on its own, but gardens are created in perfect order, according to the gardener's desires.

Your garden may have the exact plants found in a jungle. Though arrayed with artistry, it is more functional for your needs and pleasing to the eye. With the proper tools, gardeners strategically place plants in an array that encourages growth, reflects their most beautiful attributes, and reassures their tolerance from season to season. Without the right tools such as shovels, pruning shears, and mental blueprint, you cannot bring structure to a garden. Mostly, **it's not about what plants are in the garden. It is about using the tools to bring them to their proper placement.**

You may be wondering what I am building to with all of this botanical talk. Like a gardener, GOD has given you a garden, along with the tools needed to develop and manage it. HE gave you a garden (life) full of things to manage, such as family, finances, relationships, and your being (Soul,

Body, and Spirit). Among other things, He also entrusted you with intelligence, talents, education, and intuitive abilities- all of which are considered tools.

In-kind with the plant garden, **do not focus on what is out of order in your life (garden), but on using your tools to bring things into their proper placement.** Said another way, **your focus should be on managing your tools so you can best manage your garden.**

Let's have a look at a famous biblical garden. In the 2nd chapter of Genesis in the Judeo-Christian Bible it records:

> *4 On the day the Lord God made Earth and sky— 5 before any wild plants appeared on the Earth, and before any field crops grew, because the Lord God hadn't yet sent rain on the Earth and there was still no human being to farm the fertile land,6 though a stream rose from the Earth and watered all of the fertile land the Lord God formed the human[d] from the topsoil of the fertile land[e] and blew life's breath into his nostrils. The human came to life. 8 The Lord God planted a garden in Eden in the east and put there the human he had formed. 9 In the fertile land, the Lord God grew every beautiful tree with edible fruit, and also he grew the tree of life in the middle of the garden and the tree of the knowledge of good and evil.*
>
> *15 The Lord God took the human and settled him in the garden of Eden to cultivate and keep it.*

Here are a few thoughts to consider:

1. GOD withheld growth fostering rain since no one was available to farm the land (sow and reap the crops). GOD continues to operate by the principle of releasing the most significant blessings when willing and capable people are available to manage them. Ultimately, many

years later, a shipbuilder named Noah would demonstrate his ability to manage rain. As an intuitive person your job is to accurately identify tools and their purposes, in your life and in others to foster greater degrees of management met by higher degrees of blessing;
2. GOD made a garden. Isn't that marvelous? Because He is a GOD of order, HE planted a garden. As an intuitive person listening to the voice of GOD, you can become a person who benefits from the beauty of orderly management;
3. GOD took Adam out of a dry place where there was disorganization and set him in an area of order and growth. It is the will of GOD that every aspect of your life produces growth in one form or fashion. Throughout life, you may experience various seasons of disorder. These times are often fashioned for your development, not loss. While we cannot always trace the hand of GOD, we must trust HIS heart; and
4. GOD told Adam to "cultivate and "keep" the garden HE planted (Genesis 2:15). "Cultivate" would suggest making something better, and "keep" would suggest protecting. In retrospect, GOD told Adam, here is the beautiful place that I have created for you, make it better, and guard it.

GOD has given you a garden along with the tools to improve and defend it. Without hearing from GOD, it is nearly impossible to manage your territory. As we know from Adam's fall from Eden, **what doesn't get managed, gets lost**. No one likes to lose.

Character-Based Management > Talents and Intuitive Abilities

There are multitudes of people with money, talent, supernatural ability, and personal influence who do not prevail in their endeavours. Why? **Management often separates those who succeed from those who do not. The one** who has the character to bring their gifts and resources into management will succeed. Management is only as capable as the character which supports it. I encourage you to **celebrate character more than you celebrate gifts.**

In Matthew's 25th chapter of the Judeo-Christian Bible, he records Jesus' "parable of the talents." In the parable, the master gave three people "talents." Out of three people, only two of them were able to multiply their talents, while the other remained stagnant. Each one of them was given gifts, and only some were able to manage them appropriately. As with a vehicle, a manufacturer knows the purposes and proper usage of its functions. GOD knows you. GOD created you. Leveraging your intuitive ability to listen to GOD will enable you to manage the territory given to you effectively.

With such a sobering explanation, I am sure you are further encouraged to manage what you've been given. **It takes intuitive listening, led by the Holy Spirit, to know:**
1. **what your garden is supposed to look like;**
2. **identify what tools you have been equipped with;**
3. **when to use your tools;**
4. **how to use your tools; and**
5. **with whom to share your tools.**

What to Take Away From This Section

You should now understand that organizational management is one of the critical functions of your purpose on Earth.

Key Points From Section 1

1. GOD speaks with intention and purpose. If you evolve into a person of intention and purpose, HE will talk to you more frequently.
2. It's not about what plants are in the garden. It is about using the tools to bring them to their proper placement. The focus should not be on what is out of order in your life (garden), but about using your tools to bring things into their proper placement. Managing your tools aides you in managing your garden.
3. As it was with Adam in the Garden of Eden and the servant with his talents, what doesn't get managed, gets lost.
4. Management can determine success or failure. Those who have the character to bring their gifts and resources into management will often succeed.
5. Management is only as capable as the character which supports it. Mature, intuitive people celebrate character more than gifts. Gifts are given, character is developed over time.
6. GOD-inspired intuitive listening tells us what our gardens are supposed to look like, what tools you are equipped with, when to use your tools, how to use your tools, and with whom to share your tools.

Section 2: Intrinsic Personal Authority

Your Authorization to Manage Your Domain

One fundamental premise which must be driven regarding hearing from GOD is that HE speaks with purpose. **A purpose-driven life = hearing from GOD.** GOD speaks more frequently to those who understand HIS ways and are working with HIM. You may be saying to yourself, do I need to know all of this to hear from GOD? Yes. In this chapter, I must establish a strong foundation in three areas: (1)why you need to hear from GOD, (2) your source for hearing GOD, and (3) what to do once you hear from Him.

In chapter 2, we identified that the Holy Spirit speaks and works in tandem with your Spirit. Now let's take things a step deeper by exchanging the term "garden" for "personal-domain." Domain refers to a region, realm, or territory. Hence, **your personal domain is the specific region, realm, or territory that you were given by GOD to protect and cultivate.** Among other areas, tour personal-domain includes your family, job or business, Body, and Soul, among many other areas.

GOD speak to you regarding your personal domain, mainly because it was HIS purpose for you to manage it. **GOD always provides you with an architectural blueprint revealing the intended design for your personal domain**. According to King Solomon, in the 20th chapter of Proverbs of the Judeo-Christian Bible, "the purposes of a man's heart are deep waters, and the righteous know how to draw them out."

Through salvation, the Holy Spirit instantaneously engrafts with your Spirit so that it can be considered righteous in the eyes of GOD. **The Holy Spirit provides you with the ability to extract the architectural blueprint for your personal-domain out of the dimension we call eternity.** GOD speaks in dimensions, and sometimes the blueprint is challenging to decode. Understanding both the simple and complex occurs only through intuitive inspiration by the Holy Spirit.

Now that you understand personal domain, let us look at how we can manage it. We can define authority as the power and right delegated to you. **Personal authority is the gifting and ability given by GOD for an individual to fulfill their purpose on the Earth.**

One of the most significant reasons people miss hearing GOD concerns the relationship between personal authority and personal domain. Why? Jesus spent nearly 70% of His time on Earth engaging spiritual adversaries. Momentarily we will discuss these powerful, interdimensional beings fixated on halting the expression of GOD'S love. Considering they are incapable of hindering GOD, they engage HIS earthly vessels, humanity.

Please understand, **you are not being distracted from hearing GOD. You are being distracted from hearing GOD's instructions on exercising your personal authority over your personal domain.** Without intuitive listening, we relegate ourselves to the laws of this three-dimensional world. Remember, the supernatural only partners with the supernatural. Hopefully, this sheds light on why it is so hard for you to hear from GOD.

Authority is intrinsic. Every person or living thing receives the gifting and ability to fulfill their authority over their personal domain. The tree has the intrinsic authority to harvest the sun and bear fruit. The bird has the intrinsic authority to navigate and mount the wind. I hope the use of the word intrinsic causes you to consider that GOD pre-wired you with the personal-authority needed to achieve.

3 Steps to Activating Personal Authority

You merely have to activate the personal authority GOD gave you to impact your purpose or personal domain. Now do not forget, a purpose-driven life =hearing from GOD. Engaging GOD to determine HIS purpose for your life will almost always strike up a rightfully placed conversation. Let us look at three ways to activate our personal authority.

1. **Identification of Personal Authority and Domain:** Gifts are not made, but discovered. Once gifts are discovered, they should be cultivated. Seeking your personal authority and domain will activate intuitive communication with the Holy Spirit.
2. **Employment of Personal Authority:** Once you have identified your personal authority, you must exercise it within the platform given to you by GOD. Often, while you work on your personal domain, GOD will allow you to employ your personal authority for others. Building the personal domain of another becomes one of your assignments to exercise personal authority. The principle will likely not encourage excitement in your natural Soul. Nevertheless, GOD employs your personal authority for others to promote self-discovery and the development of the character-based management skills needed to complete the construction of your personal domain.
3. **Union of Personal Authority:** GOD has caused the world to be interrelated. The Earth needs the sun and moon, cells need atoms, and we need each other. However, this step often becomes a roadblock for many as it requires selflessly working with others despite differences. **Personal authority is always interrelated and dependent upon the personal authority of others**. Though they doubted Him, Jesus needed the personal authority of His disciples. **Humanity was designed to be an orchestra, not a solo performance.** Your personal domain (family, business, etc) will likely not reach maturity absent cooperation from others. GOD encourages us to identify the people HE established within our sphere to collectively employ personal authority. This final step to activating your

Personal authority is also the first step in establishing higher levels of personal domain and authority.

Although GOD can speak regarding all matters of your life, do not settle for only hearing from HIM in times of crisis. With the renewed understanding that GOD speaks with intention and purpose, focus on living a life of intention and purpose. Seek GOD regularly on the proper application of your personal authority and domain. This simple principle will restore your intrinsic, intuitive nature.

What to Take Away From This Section

You should now know GOD speaks with intention and purpose. Engaging GOD on how to use your personal authority to impact your personal domain will encourage intuitive, purpose-driven conversations with your Creator.

Key Points From Section 2

1. GOD speaks more frequently to those who understand HIS ways and are working with HIM. A purpose-driven life = hearing from GOD.
2. Your personal domain is the specific region, realm, or territory that you were given by GOD to protect and cultivate. Among many other areas, this includes your family, job or business, Body and Soul, among many other areas.
3. GOD always provides you with an architectural blueprint revealing the intended design for your personal domain.
4. The Holy Spirit provides you with the ability to extract the architectural blueprint for your personal domain out of the dimension we call eternity.
5. Personal authority is the gifting and ability given by GOD for an individual to fulfill their purpose on the Earth. External influences hope to distract you from hearing GOD's instructions on how to exercise your personal authority over your personal domain.
6. Authority is intrinsic. Every person or living thing receives the gifting and ability to fulfill their authority over their personal domain.
7. The three steps to activating personal authority are (1) Identification of Personal Authority and Domain, (2) Employment of Personal Authority and (3) Union of Personal Authority.
8. Personal authority is interrelated, depending upon the Personal authority of others.

9. Jesus' disciples doubted Him, but He still leveraged their personal authority to advance His message.

Chapter 4

Partnering With The Premier Intuitive Guide

Dimensions and Operations of The Holy Spirit

Section 1: Your Most Valuable Relationship

The Holy Spirit, Your Guide to Intuitive Listening

Kathryn Kuhlman, one of the greatest intuitive operators of our time, stated, "there are literally thousands and thousands in the great charismatic movement who have never become acquainted with the person of the Holy Spirit, only with His gift," a *Glimpse into Glory 2000*. **The Holy Spirit is more than a figment of our imagination. He is more than just a force of power. He does more than seal your eternal destiny with GOD. Shortly, you will learn that He is your Counsellor, Source, Caretaker, and Confidant.**

Considering this book is about hearing from GOD, it is essential to underscore that, The Holy Spirit is your most valuable relationship as it relates to GOD speaking to and through you. Many do not realize that the Holy Spirit is the voice of GOD and do not emphasize His deity or importance. **Relationship with the Holy Spirit=Hearing from GOD.** In Paul's 5th letter to the Galatians of the Judeo-Christian Bible, he writes, "since we are living by the Spirit, let us follow the Spirit's leading in every part of our lives." To follow Paul's guidance of trusting the intuitive leading of the Holy Spirit, we must first know of and have a relationship with Him.

Christians often reference the leading of the Holy Spirit while explaining their actions or outcomes. Truthfully, we often unconsciously follow the voice of our Soul (natural mind, will, emotions, and intellect), mistakenly representing communication with The Holy Spirit. **Our relationship with the Holy Spirit is metaphysical, outside of the natural human senses.** Connection and comprehension with The Holy Spirit occur through our Spirit. It is imperative you capably differentiate the "voice" of your mind, from that of The Holy Spirit.

When you dedicate your life to Jesus, The Holy Spirit comes in to "communion" by joining with your

Spirit. Communion is the sharing of intimate thoughts and feelings.

Once in communion with The Holy Spirit, your job is to continually ask Him for guidance in "perfectly deploying" your personal authority, through developing your Soul and Body. Jesus promised His followers that The Holy Spirit would come to guide them in "ALL TRUTH" and that He would only speak what He hears from GOD. **Once you have heard from the Holy Spirit, you have heard from GOD.**

32 Operations of The Holy Spirit

Once you can hear His voice, The Holy Spirit will play many roles in your life. For instance, He can provide intuitive guidance in speech. Is your memory unreliable? Are you concerned you will not have the right things to say? In John's 14th chapter of the Judeo-Christian Bible, Jesus said, "The Holy Spirit will help us bring in to remembrance, the things we've learned about GOD." To operate within this intuitive recollection, you must remain in communion with The Holy Spirit. You must trust that He will provide you with the right words at the right moment. Are you having a hard time telling the difference between right and wrong? The Holy Spirit provides intuitive support in decision making and moral judgment. Jesus calls The Holy Spirit a Counsellor who will guide us in our everyday lives. **GOD desires us to rid ourselves of decisions and in- fluences adversely impacting our personal domain.** When our original purpose is deterred, GOD's desires are deterred. When GOD's desires are deterred, people often create environments that hurt others.

The Holy Spirit works from our Spirit to our Soul, making us aware of the proper course for our lives. Your mind, will, intellect, and emotions transform as you carefully attend to His words of advice and correction. Conceptually, this is the basis for the Christian term "renewing of the mind." What is the best way to communicate with GOD, you ask? The Holy Spirit supports in inter-dimensional communication with GOD. Through many of his writings, Apostle Paul tells us that the Holy Spirit helps us pray.

More than merely telling us what to pray, **The Holy Spirit intervenes for us by intuitively releasing prayers from our Spirit, through our Souls to be delivered by our mouths (Bodies).** The Holy Spirit not only inspires prayer through your original language but in languages non-native to you. When we agree by faith, He disengages the interference of the Soul, to pray the perfect will of GOD for your life. This happens frequently when The Holy Spirit is not only living in you but delivering power through you. Below you will learn more about our general levels of relationships with The Holy Spirit.

According to the Judeo-Christian Bible, below are you will find 32 common ways The Holy Spirit to partners with those who receive Him.

1) Provides Access to GOD-Eph. 2:18
2) Establishes Personal-authority-Luke 4:18
3) Provides Assurance-Gal. 4:6
4) Authors Scripture-2 Pet. 1:20-21
5) Baptizes-1 Cor. 12:13-14
6) Establishes Salvation-John 3:3-6
7) Commissions Assignments-Acts 13:24
8) Cleanses Souls-1 Thess. 3:13
9) Convicts of Wrongdoing-John 16:9
10) Creates-Gen. 1:2
11) Empowers-1 Thess. 1:5
12) Communes With Human Spirits-Acts 4:29
13) Gives Supernatural Ability-I Cor. 12:8
14) Authenticates Jesus-John 16:14
15) Guides in Truth-John 16:13
16) Helps in Times of Weakness-Rom. 8:26
17) Inspires Prayer-Eph. 6:18
18) Intervenes -Rom. 8:26

19) Interprets-1 Cor. 2:1
20) Leads-Rom. 8:14
21) Liberates-Rom. 8:2
22) Molds Morality-Gal. 5:18
23) Produces Character-Gal. 5:22
24) Empowers Believers-Luke 24:49
25) Stops Eternal Death-Rom. 8:11
26) Regenerates-Titus 3:5
27) Renews Souls -Rom. 15:16
28) Seals Salvation-Eph. 1:13
29) Strengthens-Eph. 3:16
30) Teaches-John 14:26
31) Testifies of Jesus-John 15:26
32) Leads Intimacy w/GOD-Phil. 3:3

4 Dimensions of Relationship with The Holy Spirit

In John's 14th chapter of the Judeo-Christian Bible, Jesus said "The Spirit of truth (The Holy Spirit), whom the world cannot receive, because it sees Him not, neither knows Him: but you know him; for he dwells **with you**, and shall be **in you.** From here, we find the first two relational dimensions of The Holy Spirit as He (1) "dwells with you" and (2) "lives in you." In the 2nd chapter of Luke's Book of Acts, of the Judeo-Christian Bible Jesus' disciples went to Jerusalem to pray, fast, and wait for the third level of relationship with The Holy Spirit.

According to this account, after a while, they were gathered together, and the Holy Spirit rested **upon them**, evidenced by instant supernatural abilities. Here we get the third relational dimension with The Holy Spirit when He (3) "rests upon you." Remember, our relationship with The Holy Spirit is meta- physical and beyond natural explanation. The "directional positions" used to describe our relationship with Him are not physical. Instead, the content and purpose of each relationship level should be understood. Let's look closely at each relational dimension with the Holy Spirit.

1. **He Dwells With You (First-Dimension)**: The term "dwells with you" describes that The Holy Spirit is in your company, by your side. When someone accompanies you, they walk next to you. This relationship level with The Holy Spirit is the experience of those who have not yet decided to follow Jesus. The Holy Spirit walks beside them, encouraging the pursuit of their true identity in relationship with their Creator.

2. **He Lives In You (Second-Dimension)**: The term "lives in you" refers to when The Holy Spirit moves from the outside to the inside. This level occurs when a person dedicates their life to following Jesus. **The Holy Spirit represents the heart, mind, and power of Jesus. When you accept Jesus, He lawfully sends The Holy Spirit to live with your Spirit.** When the Holy Spirit lives in a person, they receive eternal salvation. They also gain the ability to renew their Souls into the character of GOD known in Christian terms as the "Fruits of The Holy Spirit."(Galatian 5:22-23)

3. **He Rests Upon You (Third-Dimension)**: The term "rest upon you" refers to when the power of The Holy Spirit surrounds you. Jesus told His disciples, "You shall receive power after the Holy Spirit comes upon you" (Acts 1:7). In Christian terms, this is known as the "Baptism of The Holy Spirit." When the Holy Spirit rests upon you, your intuitive abilities and gifts activated, as you will learn shortly.

4. **He Lives Through You (Fourth-Dimension):** This is the highest dimension of relationship with The Holy Spirit, known as "Sonship." This is when GOD is able to express HIMSELF through you 24-hours a day because your human Soul is in alignment with the Holy Spirit. There is a certain "Glory" associated with this di-

mension that can only be grasped in maturity. For now, let's try to embrace the often misunderstood third-dimension of relationship with the Holy Spirit.

The Third-Dimension of Relationship With The Holy Spirit

The lives of Jesus' disciples are the best case studies for radical transformation. Before their supernatural encounter, they were scared, abrasive, reliant upon their natural understanding, and incapable of comprehending scriptures written about their leader. That all changed once the Holy Spirit rested upon them. Contrary to other religious leaders, Jesus provided His followers with supernatural support in His physical absence.

As described in John's 16th chapter of the Judeo-Christian Bible, Jesus advised His disciples He would send the Holy Spirit, providing them the same supernatural abilities He demonstrated. Jesus remained faithful to His word. In every chapter of his Book of Acts, Luke the physician, references an abundance of miracles committed by Jesus' followers. **The third-dimension of relationship with The Holy Spirit empowered the disciples to prove the authenticity of Jesus to the world.**

Though Jesus and His followers lived their lives in partnership with The Holy Spirit, many today do not have a concept of a relationship with Him. Modern Christianity often focuses only on salvation (the second-dimension of relationship with The Holy Spirit). According to Luke's 8th chapter of the Book of Acts, in the Judeo-Christian Bible Jesus' senior disciples believed salvation was only the beginning of the Christian experience:

> "^{14} *When the apostles in Jerusalem heard that Samaria had accepted the word of God, they sent Peter and John to Samaria.* ^{15} *When they arrived, they prayed for the new believers there that they might receive*

the Holy Spirit, ¹⁶ because the Holy Spirit had not yet come on any of them; they had simply been baptized in the name of the Lord Jesus. ¹⁷ Then Peter and John placed their hands on them, and they received the Holy Spirit." (Acts 8:14-17)

Peter and John were considered the senior disciples of Jesus. Likely, no one possessed a closer in-person relationship with Jesus than them. Having acknowledged the Samarians received miracles and "salvation," they still found it necessary for them to experience the "third-dimension of relationship with The Holy Spirit." Even Jesus, after water baptism, needed The Holy Spirit to rest upon Him before beginning his ministry. In Luke's writing he records:

²¹ When all the people were being baptized, Jesus was baptized too. And as he was praying, heaven was opened ²², and the Holy Spirit descended upon him in bodily form like a dove. And a voice came from heaven: "You are my Son, whom I love; with you, I am well pleased." (Luke 3:21-22)

If Peter, John, and Jesus found it necessary for people to experience the third-dimension of relationship with The Holy Spirit, then we should too. How do we enter into these mysteries dimensions of relationship with The Holy Spirit?

Shifting from the First to Second-Dimension of Relationship With The Holy Spirit

If you are truly seeking to hear from GOD with Jesus as your guide, repeat this prayer, "Jesus I believe that you are the Son of GOD, come into my life, change me, save me and make me like you, I receive you in as my Savior, Teacher, and Friend, Amen." If your words were met with belief, The Holy Spirit is living in you on behalf of Jesus.

Shifting from the Second to Third-Dimension of Relationship With The Holy Spirit

Do you want to shift from only talking about Jesus, to tangibly demonstrating Jesus' power over death? The Holy Spirit can choose to rest upon people while they are alone or through prayer with others. He will decide the best time to enrich your relationship. Jesus' disciples waited for some time after praying to receive The Holy Spirit. It may take seconds, weeks, or months for you to encounter this level of relationship. Through a heart seeking to demonstrate the nature of Jesus to the world, He will come.

If you are ready to work with GOD, use this prayer as your guide: *Jesus, I want to represent you with every gift that you have made available to me. Give me boldness in your name, for your glory. As you promised, I am calling for your Holy Spirit to rest upon me, to saturate my life and restrict all that is not like you. Holy Spirit, I ask that you would baptize me with the character and power of GOD, in the name of Jesus, Amen.*

What to Take Away From This Section

You have now learned that your intuitive ability is complete through a relationship with The Holy Spirit and that mature, intuitive people operate from the third dimension of relationship with Him.

Key Points From Section 1

1. The Holy Spirit is your most valuable relationship as it relates to GOD speaking to and through you.
2. Relationship with the Holy Spirit=Hearing from GOD. Trusting the intuitive leading of The Holy Spirit requires a relationship with Him.
3. Our relationship with The Holy Spirit is metaphysical, outside of the natural human senses.
4. When you dedicate your life to Jesus, The Holy Spirit comes into communion with you by joining with your Spirit. Communion is the sharing of intimate thoughts and feelings. Once you have heard from the Holy Spirit, you have heard from GOD.
5. The Holy Spirit works from our Spirit to our Soul, making us aware of the proper course for our lives. Your mind, will, intellect, and emotions transform as you carefully attend to His words of advice and correction.
6. The Holy Spirit performs 32 common functions in our lives.
7. There are three key relational-level with The Holy Spirit. He (1) "dwells with you" (2) "lives in you" and (3) "rests upon you."
8. The third-dimension of relationship with The Holy Spirit empowered the disciples to prove the authenticity of Jesus to the world.

Section 2: The Framework for Intuitive Listening

Decoding Intuitive Prompts From The Holy Spirit

The premise of intuitive listening centres on our being hard-wired to communicate with our Creator. **Our efforts should emphasize identifying and understanding methods of supernatural communication rather than creating our means.** We are pre-programmed to recognize circumstances that cannot be apprehended by natural human senses or even measured with time and space. All of humanity possesses metaphysical-abilities. However, the perfect methods for operating in supernatural realms are derived from and guided by The Holy Spirit through a relationship with Jesus Christ.

The Holy Spirit guides our cross-dimensional exploits. Being mission-centric, He will only allow us to move within the dimensions necessary for us to accomplish the Heart of GOD, according to the measure of our personal authority. Being a genuine caretaker as we communicate through hidden dimensions, The Holy Spirit guards us against exposure to information we are not mature enough to receive. Plainly said, The Holy Spirit will protect you from spiritual encounters that will cause you unnecessary trauma.

Sometimes we pray for a definitive answer. However, if the revelation were received, we could not contain it. Why would GOD expose us to matters before our maturation? GOD is the model of intention and purpose. **GOD does not give us what we pray for, but what we can manage.** Now that you are better acquainted with the works and mission of The Holy Spirit, let's look closely at six intuitive vehicles He uses to guide us.

The 6 Major Intuitive Prompts From The Holy Spirit

Everyone possesses the ability to communicate with GOD. The Holy Spirit is tasked with serving as an intermediary between GOD and humanity. He accomplishes His assignment by interacting with us through these following six intuitive prompts:

1. **Intuitive-Confirmation (Inner-Witness):** From my experiences in coaching people, this is the most common form by which The Holy Spirit communicates to people. In Romans 9, it is written, "I tell you the truth in Christ, I am not lying, my conscience also bearing me witness in the Holy Spirit." Here the Apostle Paul is saying that he knew it is not just his brain devising words because The Holy Spirit was confirming his thoughts. Through intuitive-confirmation, The Holy Spirit provides us with a profound assurance. Some refer to an inner-witness as a "gut feeling." We should deviate from this terminology. In addition to your Spirit, the Soul and Body have their idea of what direction to take, as you will learn in chapter 7. **Intuitive-confirmation describes undoubtedly knowing without the Soul's need for direct knowledge.** In a moment's notice, your Spirit can receive an immediate conviction of right or wrong-doing. Your mind and intellect (functions of the Soul) may not rationalize the reasoning behind your affirmation, but perceive the communication from your Spirit as feelings of sureness and peace.
2. **Intuitive-Recollection (Remembrance): Through intuitive recollection, The Holy Spirit instantaneously reminds you of a conversation, circumstance, or learned knowledge at a time you need it most.** Through supernatural remembrance, you may suddenly see images in your mind or

presentation of thoughts from the past. Through intuitive-recollection, The Holy Spirit provides you with answers to decisions or dilemmas that you or others may be facing.

3. **Intuitive-Prompting (Hastening): Intuitive-prompting is experienced when The Holy Spirit rapidly projects images or intuitive sound towards you at a speed that requires your attention.** For instance, while reading, you may hone in on content that nearly "jump off the pages," causing an excitement deep within you. This form of hastening may also come in the form of a single word. You may suddenly hear (subconsciously) the word "contract" while speaking with someone who unknown to you, is in the midst of business negotiations. The meaning of the prompt must be examined to determine its purpose. Many reference The Holy Spirit intuitively-prompting them with scriptures to solve problems or provide com- fort.

4. **Intuitive-Guidance (Leadings):** Jesus, our model, was led by The Holy Spirit as He navigated life on our Earth. The scripture reads, "Then Jesus was led up by the Spirit into the wilderness..." (Matt. 4:1). **When intuitive-guidance is activated, The Holy Spirit fixates your attention away from or towards a specific area.** In forward movement, the experience compares to tunnel vision. Your Soul will perceive the Spirit-inspired, leading as an unusual attraction to a particular path. If GOD does not want you to move forward, you will experience unsettledness or unusual silence from The Holy Spirit. This expression should cause you to wait before for instructions before making further advances. Mature prophetic people, consistently seek intuitive-guidance to avoid circumstances which could cause harm. **The more that you inquire of**

the Holy Spirit will be the more opportunities that you provide for Him to speak.

5. **Dimensional-Perceptions (Visions):** In the Book of Joel the stage is set for the remaining intuitive prompts recording, "And it shall come to pass afterward that I will pour out My Spirit on all flesh; Your sons and your daughters shall prophesy, your old men shall dream dreams, your young men shall see visions..." (Joel 2:28). Note that both visions and dreams are connected to The Holy Spirit. **The two basic dimensional-perceptions that you can receive from the Holy Spirit are known as *open-visions* or *closed-visions*.** The most common dimensional-perception is that of closed-visions. **Closed-visions occur when our mind receives detailed visualizations of past, present, or future events.** Those who have experienced closed-visions describe the event as The Holy Spirit projecting movies directly towards to their mind. **The second dimensional-perception is that of open-visions. These encounters are experienced when The Holy Spirit takes you out of our three-dimensional realm to experience an important event.** John, the author of the Book of Revelation, experienced an open-vision of future events.

6. **Subconscious-Intervention (Dreams):** People all over the world receive direct communication from GOD through subconscious-intervention. **Biblically referred to as "visions of the night," supernatural dreams are messages delivered by The Holy Spirit while your Soul is at rest.** This topic is addressed further in chapter 7.

What to Take Away From This Section

You have now established a firm foundation for hearing from GOD. The six intuitive-prompts of The Holy Spirit will be your general platform for intuitive operation.

Key Points From Section 2

1. Our studies in intuitive listening should emphasize identifying and understanding methods of communication rather than creating our means.
2. GOD does not give us what we pray for, but what we can manage.
3. The Holy Spirit guides our cross-dimensional exploits allowing us to move within the measure of our personal-authority. As we move through spiritual realms, The Holy Spirit guards us against exposure to harmful information or acts.
4. The Holy Spirit communicates through six general, intuitive prompts.
5. The two basic dimensional-perceptions that you can receive from the Holy Spirit are known as "open-visions" or "closed-visions."
6. Supernatural dreams are messages delivered by The Holy Spirit while your Soul is at rest. Dreams are "visions of the night."

Chapter 5

Releasing Dormant Intuitive Abilities

Opening, Managing and Deploying Spiritual Gifts

Section 1: Reinstating Intuitive Function

A Child's Story of Unopened Gifts

One day when a young boy's mother took him to store, it was as though the heavens opened for him. The boy's attention fixated on a big brown fighter pilot's jacket. Although they lived in the South Florida heat, he just had to have the coat. He told his mother how much this jacket meant and that without out it, he would die (figuratively speaking). His mother looked down and said, "you know what, if you like this jacket so much I am sure your cousin would love it. Besides, his family cannot afford to buy a jacket like this for him. Don't you think that would be a better idea for us to buy it for him?"

After hearing his mother's suggestion, he began to cry and was upset with her for weeks. Finally, it was Christmas morning, and he had opened all of his gifts. His mood was grateful, yet somber because he wanted that fighter pilot jacket. The boy thanked his parents, dropped his head low, and walked away. Suddenly as she pointed towards the tree, his mother called out to him, saying, "You missed a gift!" The young man rushed over and tore the wrapping apart. Behold! There it was! The fighter pilot jacket was there!

The moral of the story, the gift was lying on the floor for weeks, unopened, without the boy realizing it was his. It was intended for him all along. He did not know it. His mother knew that it would bring him great joy, so she made sure that it was safe and tucked away until the right time. Likewise, GOD purchased and set aside your intuitive gifts in a safe place for you. Therefore, it is not a matter of whether you have gifts. Instead, it is a matter of you identifying and opening what GOD has given you.

At their loss, many have unopened gifts that lay dormant. **Unopened Gifts = Unwrapped Potential**. The gifts are already inside of us, and The Holy Spirit is our guide in unlocking them. What prevents people from finding and operating in their gifts?

Internal Influences	**External Influences**
Doubt that intuitive gifts exist	Taught to deny intuitive gifts
Doubt GOD bestows extraordinary gifts to ordinary people	Prevented from using gifts
Fear of the gifts in operation	Gifts were not identified or cultivated
Doubt their gifts are desired or needed	Capacity and abilities were misdiagnosed

4 Principles of Managing Your Wealth of Gifts

You cannot manage a garden without the proper tools. As outlined in chapter 3, GOD has given everyone domain to be managed through their personal authority. Your GOD-given gifts fall under the jurisdiction of your personal authority. GOD views supernatural gifts as valuable tools to be managed and deployed. Jesus offers a story in the Book of Matthew 25:14-29 on GOD'S desires for humanity to manage the resources given to them:

Again, it will be like a man going on a journey, which called his servants and entrusted his wealth to them. To one he gave five bags of gold, to another two bags, and to another one bag, each according to his ability. Then he went on his journey. The man who had received five bags of gold went at once and put his money to work and gained five bags more. So also, the one with two bags of gold gained two more. But the man who had received one bag went off, dug a hole in the ground and hid his master's money.

After a long time, the master of those servants returned and settled accounts with them. The man who had received five bags of gold brought the other five. Master, he said, you entrusted me with five bags of gold. See, I have gained five more. His master replied, 'Well done, good and faithful servant! <u>You have been faithful with a few things; I will put you in charge of many things</u>.' Come and share your master's happiness!"

The man with two bags of gold also came. Master, he said, you entrusted me with two bags of gold; see, I have gained two more. His master replied, 'Well done, good and faithful servant! You have been faithful with a few things; I will put you in charge of many things.' Come and share your master's happiness!

Then the man who had received one bag of gold came. Master, he said, I knew that you are a hard man, harvesting where you have not sown and gathering where you have not scattered seed. So I was afraid and went out and hid your gold in the ground. See, here is what belongs to you. His master replied, 'you wicked, lazy servant! So you knew that I harvest where I have not sown and gather where I have not scattered seed?

Well then, you should have put my money on deposit with the bankers, so that when I returned, I would have received it back with interest.' So take the bag of gold from him and give it to the one who has ten bags. <u>For whoever has will be given more, and they will have abundance. Whoever does not have, even what they have will be taken from them</u>.

There are four principal considerations to be gained from the parable: (1) GOD has entrusted you with great wealth, (2) GOD distributes wealth according to our abilities, (3) GOD provides additional wealth to those who need it; and (4) GOD de- signed you to be driven by purpose, not fear. Look closely at each principle.

Principle #1: GOD has entrusted you with great wealth. It is important to know that GOD has assigned wealth to humankind. Have you ever considered the difference between the terms "rich" and "wealthy"? In most developed societies, the term "rich" almost always denotes the abundance of money. However, the term "wealth" is far more expansive than what initially meets the eye. I describe "wealth" as **the abundance of valuable resources an individual possesses for bettering society.** In theory, you may intrinsically possess a wealth of inventions, solutions to significant problems, or wisdom that could connect divided people-groups. **Your** Creator endowed you *with* a wealth of gifts for use.

Principal #2 GOD distributes wealth according to our abilities. In Jesus' parable, the master gave bags according to the measure of each man's ability. Jesus' statements suggest an unequal distribution of gifts and skills. Remember, your intuitive abilities are unmerited. GOD pre-wired you with everything needed to accomplish your purpose.

Principal #3 GOD provides additional wealth to those who need it. In the parable above, the master tells the men who doubled their talents, that their trustworthy custodianship over a little, will grant them with a lot. **GOD does not give more to those who ask, HE gives more to those who have adequately managed what HE has provided.** We often squander the little bit we have then audaciously ask for more. GOD functions in order, purpose, and management. We must demonstrate our ability to be good custodians for GOD to place more under our charge.

Principal #4 GOD designed you to be driven by purpose, not fear. The third servant mentioned in the parable who received one bag was afraid the master did not have a safe investment strategy and buried the gold. GOD did not design us to be fearful. Minus the servants fear he would likely have acted wisely just as his counterparts did. Many know of their gifts, but are too afraid to use them. Like the servant, some believe GOD made the wrong investment by choosing them. We should not let fear hold us back from being whom GOD created us to be. **When GOD bestowed you with person- al domain and authority, HE gave you a license to be authentic. Many come into this world as originals and**

leave as copies. Be an original and leave an original, without fear.

Balancing the Terms Spiritual, Intuitive, Supernatural and Metaphysical

The expression "spiritual gifts" is used by the Apostle Paul throughout the Judeo-Christian Bible. The term is derived from the Greek word "charismata," defining the power of The Holy Spirit, which "rests upon" an individual to serve GOD through extraordinary means. "Rests upon" implies the third-dimension of relationship with The Holy Spirit, as outlined in chapter 4. Even Jesus, after water baptism, needed The Holy Spirit to rest upon Him before beginning his ministry. At a moment's notice, The Holy Spirit can supernaturally intervene by activating your spiritual gifts.

Being made in the image of GOD (our Spirits), all humanity possesses spiritual gifts. GOD has delivered them to us without regret. The deployment of a person's spiritual gifts is determined by the "free will" of their Souls. To avoid doubt, **Spiritual Gifts= Intuitive Abilities = Metaphysical Abilities = Supernatural Abilities. When governed by The Holy Spirit, the descriptions have the same meaning.** We often reject what we do not understand or accept. This book attempts to balance spiritual and natural terms through scientific and religious means. **Our definitions often determine our expectations.** Do not accept or reject an idea based on a mere word. Investigate all relevant matters with your natural and spiritual gifts before arriving at a definition.

What to Take Away From This Section

You should now understand there are various classifications used to describe your nature. Your job is to overcome definitions to achieve self-discovery.

Key Points From Section 1

1. Unopened Gifts=Unwrapped Potential.
2. There are four principles of managing gifts are (1) GOD has entrusted you with great wealth; (2) GOD distributes wealth according to our abilities; (3) GOD provides additional wealth to those who need it; and (4) GOD designed you to be driven by purpose, not fear.
3. The word "Wealth" can be described as the abundance of valuable resources an individual possesses for bettering society. All of our abilities are considered wealth by GOD.
4. GOD does not give more to those who ask; HE gives more to those who have adequately managed what HE has provided.
5. When GOD bestowed you with personal domain and authority, HE gave you a license to be authentic. Many come into this world as originals and leave as copies.
6. The expression "spiritual gifts" is derived from the Greek word "charismata," defining the power of The Holy Spirit, which "rests upon" an individual to serve GOD through extraordinary means.
7. Spiritual Gifts = Intuitive Abilities = Metaphysical Abilities = Supernatural Abilities. When governed by The Holy Spirit, the descriptions have the same meaning.

Section 2: The Purpose of Intuitive Gifts

Becoming an Ambassador of Heaven

The term "intuitive communication" involves gathering and delivering information between multiple dimensions. In chapter 4, you identified six common vehicles used by The Holy Spirit to communicate. **Through intuitive partnership with GOD, you can act as an ambassador of the dimension of Heaven.** GOD uses a variety of means to direct you through the maze of establishing your personal domain. As an ambassador of Heaven, HE works with you to do the same for others. GOD speaks more frequently as we guide others through the twists and turns of iden- tifying their purpose.

To create frequent opportunities to hear from GOD, we must frequently seek opportunities to be used on behalf of GOD to benefit others. Our emphasis should be on being "used on behalf of GOD." When presented, many will tend to the physical and emotional needs of others on their account. As led, recipients of your care should understand that because of HIS love, GOD sent you there to attend to their needs. We cannot give what we do not have. GOD is the Giver of our gifts and resources.

When you serve others on your behalf, you receive the reward of gratitude from the recipient. When you serve others on behalf of GOD, you receive the reward of gratitude from GOD. Our motivation for use determines our source of reward. **Mature, intuitive communicators are waiters, and GOD is their chef.** Waiters place orders, but chefs control what leaves the kitchen. They do not take credit for what is served. They simply deliver what the chef prepared.

When a person obtains Heavenly information, they have received the supernatural gift of "revelation." The gift should not be tampered with. **A revelation is knowledge of the pro-

tocol, processes, and purposes of Heaven from Earth. Revelation provides ambassadors of Heaven with a section of GOD'S blueprint for individuals and the world's communities. **Revelation is often an invitation to power.** Communicating the mind of GOD is good. Demonstrating the Mind of GOD is better.

More than communication, your intrinsic authority provides supernatural power to physically and tangibly help the world. Mature, intuitive people understand their purpose is not to fulfill every desire, but to support blueprints given by GOD. As a reminder, **a purpose-driven life=Hearing from GOD**. Seek understanding of GOD's purpose before using supernatural gifts. Seeking opportunities to fulfill the seven assignments below, you will provide GOD with more opportunities to speak and partner with you.

7 Assignments For Intuitive Communicators

When fulfilling the purpose of our intuitive tools, The Holy Spirit extracts communication, solutions, and instructions from Heaven for ambassadors to bring it into the natural world. Seven everyday assignments of intuitive communication include (1) declaring the heart and will of GOD; (2) identifying the intuitive nature of others; (3) interpreting messages from GOD; (4) encouraging the discouraged; (5) providing sound counsel and instruction; (6) comforting those in need; and (7) demonstrating morality to the world. Let's look closely at common assignments for intuitive communicators.

1. **Declaring the Heart and Will of GOD.** Through intuitive communication, our assignment is to identify areas preventing others from coming into a relationship with GOD. Many in the world have misconceptions about GOD and the gift HE gave in the form of Jesus. According to John 3, GOD desires the entire world to come into a relationship with HIM. Mature, intuitive people focus

on serving as ambassadors between GOD and HIS intention of restoring humankind. The most excellent demonstration of GOD'S Heart should be witnessed in daily life. **More than verbal expression, Love is an act of demonstration.**

2. **Identifying the Intuitive Nature of Others:** Through intuitive communication, our assignment is to reveal the supernatural abilities placed into others by GOD. With accurate perception, an intuitive person can pinpoint unique abilities that allow others to manage their personal-authority and domain.

3. **Interpreting Messages from GOD:** Through intuitive communication, our assignment is to provide a bridge of connection between GOD and mankind. Ambassadors of the dimension of Heaven can reveal hidden mysteries found in the dreams, visions, and patterns of the lives of others.

4. **Encouraging the Discouraged:** Through intuitive communication, our assignment is to identify and remind those in need of GOD's ability and desire to advocate for them. People seeking to do good often experience adversity. From broken relationships to economic loss, people need encouragement more than ever. GOD has the final rule on how situations are resolved. While others navigate the winds of life, we must be uplifting, esteeming, and encouraging.

5. **Providing Sound Counsel and Instruction:** Through intuitive communication, our assignment is to provide others with precise directives from GOD. Life often presents us with complex questions about relationships, business, and health decisions, among others. Intuitive people must be confident in their ability to hear GOD and submit clear answers to difficult circumstances. When giving intuitive counsel, The Holy Spirit extracts solutions and instructions from eternity and bring it into the natural world. Supernatural advice

offers present guidance based on GOD'S knowledge of the future.

6. **Comforting Those in Need:** Through intuitive communication, our assignment is to identify and provide refuge to those who need it. When we give comfort to others, we create an opportunity to extend the Hand of GOD by providing physical and emotional rest. The assignment encouraging (above) focuses on vocally inspiring people into their destiny and purposes. In a world riddled with poverty, sickness, and hopelessness, Heaven's ambassadors tangibly provide hope in proverbial darkness.

7. **Demonstrating Morality to the World:** Through intuitive communication, our assignment is to establish and proclaim the ethical standards of GOD before others. In a world divided about issues such as "human rights," intuitive voices must weigh in with counsel from the Creator of all things. The best declaration of morality is demonstrated through our daily actions and decisions, not by what we proclaim. When others are looking for GOD, they should be able to find HIM in you.

What to Take Away From This Section

You should now understand that as an Ambassador of Heaven, your purpose is to partner with GOD in guiding others into divine purpose.

Key Points From Section 2

1. The term "intuitive communication" involves gathering and delivering information between multiple dimensions.
2. Through your intuitive partnership with GOD, you are an Ambassador of the dimension of Heaven directing direct others through the twists and turns of identifying their purpose.
3. To create frequent opportunities to hear from GOD, we must frequently seek opportunities to be used on behalf of GOD to benefit others.
4. The motivation for using spiritual gifts determines our source of reward. When you serve others on your behalf, you receive the reward of gratitude from the recipient. When you serve others on behalf of GOD, you receive the reward of gratitude from GOD.
5. Mature, intuitive communicators are waiters, and GOD is their chef. Waiters place orders, but chefs control what leaves the kitchen. They do not take credit for what is served. They simply deliver what the chef prepared.
6. A revelation is knowledge of the protocol, processes, and purposes of Heaven from Earth.
7. Seven everyday assignments of intuitive communication include (1) declaring the heart and will of GOD; (2) identifying the intuitive nature of others; (3) interpreting messages from GOD; (4) encouraging the discouraged; (5) providing sound counsel and instruction; (6) comforting those in need; and (7) demonstrating morality to the world.

Chapter 6

Understanding Intuitive Dimensions of Operation

Clarifying Spiritual Streams and Functions

Section 1: Tools of Intuitive Operation

Influencing What You Have Heard With What You Have

In this section, we will look at several supernatural gifts given to you by GOD. The Holy Spirit guides and increases your gifts when you exercise them as an agent of Heaven. Remember, revelation is often an invitation to power. **More than communication, GOD provides you with demonstrable power. Spiritual gifts empower intuitive people in the deployment of supernatural knowledge and solutions.** You are supernaturally empowered to cultivate the "gardens of the world."

Before reviewing the first list of supernatural gifts and abilities, let's revisit a few basics: The words "dimensional" or "spiritual" refer to the function of operating in multiple realms and planes of existence, beyond the naturally seen, three-dimensional world. The terms "spiritual," " intuitive," " metaphysical," and "supernatural" are generally interchangeable.

Your Spirit contains all supernatural abilities required for you to prosper on Earth. Your Spirit is the epitome of who you are. As you discover the spiritual gifts noted below, remember that the definitions are supernatural. In partnership with The Holy Spirit, your Spirit performs these extraordinary abilities. These gifts are not natural but divine in function and operation. Also, it is imperative to keep in mind that your purpose for understanding spiritual gifts must exceed self-identification. In other words, learn with the intent of identifying the gifts of others. GOD does not help those who help themselves, as much as HE helps those who help others.

Streams and Functions of 21 Common Supernatural Gifts

For additional study, the location of the supernatural gifts below is 1 Corinthians 12, Romans 12, Ephesians 4, and Isaiah 11 of the Judeo-Christian Bible. For all intended purposes, four of the Ephesians 4 gifts were not included. Further characterizations to the names of the supernatural gifts are given to reflect the depth of description. For the purposes of this book, **"spiritual streams," also known as "operation gifts" are supernatural abilities that flow continuously through your character traits. Spiritual gifts are deployed intermittently to fulfill the purpose of GOD, on a moment-by-moment basis.** Look closely to identify a few of the supernatural gifts given to humankind by GOD.

1. **Dimensional Intervention (Intercessory Prayer):** This spiritual gift allows you to impact multiple dimensions through the prompting of the Holy Spirit. People with this gift can change the world around them by declaring the Word and Will of GOD through prayer. In response, GOD releases the power to override dark circumstances. Although often overlooked, all followers of Jesus can attain and operate in this gift. Sincere prayer is inspired by the Holy Spirit to activate and release celestial forces out of the Kingdom of GOD to cause intervention over the Earth realm.

2. **Intuitive Information Reception (Word of Knowledge):** This spiritual gift reveals the needs of people through supernatural knowledge and understanding. With intuitive knowledge of the past or present (not the future), people with this gift prevent or reverse adverse situations by revealing the Heart of GOD. This gift empowers people by bringing clarity and under- standing to their lives of others. The word "knowledge" is derived from the Greek word "gnosis," which means

recognition or understanding of subject matter. This knowledge is not ascertained by natural means. The gift causes the carrier to supernaturally receive information that would be impossible to know without GOD.

3. **Intuitive Insight Reception (Word of Wisdom):** This spiritual gift allows you to supernaturally apply resolutions in a matter that can be received by those involved. People with this gift skillfully distill supernatural insight and discernment into excellent advice. The possession of information or knowledge does not guarantee successful methods of delivery. The gift of wisdom reveals the right application and the right time to release the knowledge that will support others.

4. **Dimensionally Acute Perception (Discernment):** This spiritual gift detects what is true from false and right from wrong. People with this gift quickly identify, rightfully judge, and uncover circumstances that would typically evade others. The Greek word for the gift of discernment is "diakrisis." The word describes the distinguishing, judging, or appraising a person, statement, situation, or environment. According to the Book of John 4:1-6, only two spirits types of spirits influence the world and need to be discerned: (1) The Holy Spirit, who is good, and (2) the Spirit of the Anti-Christ, who is evil. The malevolence in the world concentrates on establishing "grey areas," causing the immoral to be considered good and good to be considered immoral. GOD identifies convoluting matters through this gift.

5. **Intuitive Accumulation & Distribution (Giving):** This operation gift gives you the ability to attract, accumulate, and contribute material resources, such as money, to advance the purposes of GOD. Four functions characterize this spiritual stream: (1) the extraordinary ability to amass wealth; (2) the acuteness to know when a material need is present; (3) the intuitive wisdom to align with needs; and (4) the authentic desire to give to

others on behalf of God. Often possessed by entrepreneurial people, this gift frees followers of Jesus from material burdens.

6. **Intuitive Organizational Management (Leadership):** This operation gift allows you to identify the blueprint of GOD for a group, set and communicate goals, all while encouraging others to work together for the accomplishment of the task effectively. Three functions characterize this spiritual stream: (1) can effectively delegate tasks without manipulation or coercion; (2) can identify the unique working-abilities of individu- als; and (3) the unique capacity to establish outlets for others to operate in their gifting.

7. **Intuitive Recognition & Attendance (Serving):** This operation gift supports you in identifying and caring for the physical needs of others through a variety of means. Three functions categorize this spiritual stream: (1) the supernatural drawing to the desperate situations of others; (2) the fulfillment in meeting the needs of others; and (3) the avoidance of commendation for their contributions.

8. **Intuitive Articulation & Instruction (Teaching):** This operation gift guides you in clearly explaining and effectively apply truths. Three functions characterize this spiritual stream: (1) the supernatural capacity to accurately engage in research and organize the results for simple communication; (2) the pressing desires to bring understanding and solutions to other; and (3) the unusual ability to maintain the attention of others while providing instruction.

9. **Heightened Intuitive Perception & Dissemination (Faith):** This spiritual gift gives you the ability to perceive, trust, and have confidence in the GOD at abnormally high levels. People with this gift tend to live boldly to manifest the will of GOD. Every believer in Jesus has been given faith to receive salvation and as-

signed "a measure of faith" for them to advance their lives. However, not all believers receive this unique ability. Three functions categorize this spiritual gift: (1) extraordinary certainty to perform complicated tasks; (2) short bursts of certainty to demonstrate supernatural exploits; and (3) elongated confidence to build solutions. Those that operate in the prophetic, healing, and miracles realms (found below) have this gift in their arsenal.

There are three general dimensions of faith:

1. The Gift of Faith: Given to a select few to commence great exploits for GOD, as mentioned in the paragraph above;
2. Faith to Receive Salvation: Given to those who receive Jesus as their eternal source. GOD gives this stream of faith for people to have a revelation of Jesus and seek HIM for their eternal salvation, not to operate in the miraculous; and
3. The Measure of Faith: Unlike the Gift of Faith, this dimension is given to all humanity to fulfill their purpose. In contrast to the Faith to Receive salvation (mentioned above), the Measure of Faith is used to demonstrate your trust in GOD while on Earth. Unlike the other two streams of faith, your daily encounters with GOD will likely be tied to your Measure of Faith. This stream of faith can be increased by believing and walking with GOD, especially during trying times. The depth of your relation- ship with GOD will be revealed in times of struggle. I have witnessed average people, who do not operate in the revered Gift of Faith, used even more mightily be- cause they have increased their Measure of Faith and trust in GOD over many seasons. Seek and respond to GOD'S voice in even the little things. If you do, more

than experiencing moments, you will live a naturally supernatural life.
10. **Dimensional Phenomena (Miracles):** This spiritual gift gives you the ability to defy the laws of nature and reveal the power of GOD. People with this gift demonstrate GOD'S ability in extraordinary ways. The spiritual gift of miracles is translated into the Greek phrase "energemata dynameon," meaning "workings of powers." As with all gifts, it is subject to the divine purpose and Will of GOD as led by The Holy Spirit.
11. **Dimensional Restorations (Healings):** This spiritual gift gives you the ability to bring physical and mental healing without the necessity of natural sources. Three functions categorize this spiritual gift: (1) the extraordinary ability to detect sickness; (2) great contempt for disease; and (3) the urgent desire for eradicating illness through the Power of GOD. The term "dimensional restoration" advocates that the original intent of GOD was perfect health and that the gift restores people to HIS original plan. This spiritual gift is closely related to the gifts of faith and miracles. All supernatural gifts are to be exercised in faith, but gifts of healings involve a special measure of it. The supernatural gifts of healings are plural. From its Greek derivative, the gift is called "charismata iamaton," meaning "gifts of healings."

The gift of healings can be broken into two supernatural streams:
1. <u>Immediate healing</u>: The ability to deliver instantaneous results; and
2. <u>Gradual healing:</u> The ability to release a cure with de- layed recognition from the natural realm.

The gift of miracles creates, and the gift of healings restores. You are encouraged to commit to further self-study regarding this gift.

12. **Intermittent Prediction & Command (Gift of Prophecy):** This spiritual gift gives you the ability to periodically receive inspiration from The Holy Spirit to release redeeming and restorative proclamations. With a single declaration, people with this gift can inspire or positively change an individual life at a moment's notice. In contrast to the Office of the Prophet, this gift is only available from a moment to moment basis. The gift of prophecy is often activated when: (1) deep worship is present; (2) when the "Office of Prophecy" is present; (3) when carriers of the gift collaborate; and (4) when the gift is deployed for intercessory prayer (dimension- al intervention). Including this gift, there are four main streams related to Prophecy (Intuitive Communication. The following is listed from the lowest to the highest level of function:

1. Intuitive Communication (The Spirit of Prophecy): GOD has the ability to speak to and through all humanity, according to the Book of Joel. This basic intuitive function relegates to delivering periodic messages from GOD. Often people are unaware when the gift is in action. The gift is centered on GOD communicating with humanity, through humanity, at HIS discretion;

2. Dimensional Guidance & Prompting (The Proclaimer of Prophecy): The operation gift to receive and proclaim a message from GOD to encourage or correct others. Unlike the Gift of Prophecy, *Proclaimers* do not possess the ability to command the dimensions of time and space. This gift is further described in #13 of this list;

3. Intermittent Predication & Demand (The Gift of Prophecy): The ability to receive occasional inspiration from The Holy Spirit that foretells, provides correction and comfort, or modifies the dimensions of time and space. This gift is further described in #13 of this list; and

4. <u>Governing Predication & Demand (The Office of Prophecy)</u>: The ability to receive constant inspiration from The Holy Spirit to (1) foretell events; (2) provide correction and comfort to people and communities; and (3) lead and develop the prophetic dimension on Earth or modify time and space. This gift operates at the highest dimension of intuitive communication and operation. Due to its complexity, the gift is not further addressed in this book. Very few fall within this category. The books of Kings outlines the many exploits of those with this ability.

13. **Dimensional Guidance & Prompting (Proclaiming):** This operation gift guides you in receiving and proclaiming a message from GOD to encourage or correct others. Unlike the Gift of Prophecy and Office of the Prophet, this gift is communication orientated and does not possess the ability to command the dimensions of time and space. Five functions categorize this spiritu- al stream: (1) leads people towards intuitive purpose and destiny; (2) provides organizational correction; (3) provide moral correction; (4) provides encouragement; and (5) provides intuitive declarations to guide groups. Corrective communication made by mature "proclaimers" is absent of personal ambition. Rather, made in love, in alignment with the scripture, and judged by at least two others.

14. **Intuitive Guidance Dissemination (Counsel):** This spiritual gift gives you the ability to determine the appropriate application, timing, and tone to support others. People with this gift procure solutions through spiritual means. The gift of wisdom (#3 in the list) is deployed to general circumstances. The gift of counsel is deployed specifically to guide people.

15. **Intuitive Dialect Transmission (Supernatural Languages):** This spiritual gift gives you the ability to speak in known or unknown languages. People with this gift use supernatural language inspired by The Holy Spirit to change the atmosphere around them. Many biblical scholars admonish the Apostle Paul as a great teacher. Though, interpretations of his teachings regarding "supernatural languages," often cause division amongst readers. It's important to understand that Paul referred to the "gift of supernatural languages" as manifesting multiple forms. There are three distinct functions of Supernatural Languages (Intuitive Dialect Transmission):

1. <u>Supernatural Sign for Unbelievers in Jesus</u>: the first function manifests as a "known language" not native to the speaker but understood by the recipient. In 1 Corinthians 14:21-22, Apostle Paul writes, "In the Law, it is written: 'With other tongues and through the lips of foreigners I will speak to this people, but even then they will not listen to me, says the Lord.' Tongues, then, are a sign, not for believers but for unbelievers." His writing indicates super- natural language operation proves GOD'S operation to those in disbelief. Benefactors of the gift are astound- ed when speakers spontaneously and fluently exclaim, through a language (not native to the speaker) known to the recipient, i.e., a German supernaturally speaking Spanish to a native of Spain;

2. <u>Mysterious Prayer Language Directed to GOD</u>: the second function manifests in an "unknown" super- natural language intended for secure communication with GOD. Inspired by The Holy Spirit, the language or sounds cannot be interpreted by humankind. In 1 Corinthians 14:2, Apostle Paul states, *"For anyone who speaks in a tongue does not speak to people but God; for no one understands him,*

but he utters mysteries by the Spirit." This statement contradicts the intention of the first stream of bringing confirmation to people. The second stream is not designed to be understood by mankind. Rather, inspired by The Holy Spirit, the stream supports confidential and perfected communication with GOD and the gift's operator; and

3. <u>Communication Established for Interpretation</u>: the third function manifests as a language known or unknown, released only for interpretation. In 1 Corinthians 14:26-28, Apostle Paul writes, "If anyone speaks in a tongue, two or at the most three should speak, one at a time and someone must inter- pret. If there is no interpreter, the speaker should keep quiet in the church and speak to himself and God."

16. **Motivational Reinforcement (Exhortation):** This operation gift empowers you to motivate others by providing timely words of encouragement and consolation. This spiritual stream can be categorized by three functions: (1) pre-disposed to find potential in others; (2) drives others to reach their goals; (3) consistently opti- mistic; and (4) consistently energetic. Exhorters thrive on turning the discouraged into the encouraged.

17. **Intuitive Strength (Might):** This spiritual gift allows you to overturn intolerable situations or circumstances that overwhelm the majority. People with this gift are empowered with the explosive stamina needed to unwind hopeless situations.

18. **Intuitive Comprehension (Understanding):** The spiritual gift gives you the ability to interpret natural and spiritual matters void experiential knowledge or direct experience. Inspired by The Holy Spirit, people

with this gift can accurately comprehend complex matters.

19. **Intuitive Dialect Recognition (Interpretation of Languages):** This spiritual gift provides you with the ability to perceive, comprehend, and recite languages unknown to you, as the gift holder. People with this gift speak the mysteries of GOD by interpreting known and supernatural languages.

20. **Intuitive Devotion (Reverence for GOD):** This spiritual gift empowers you to remain deeply concerned and submissive to the HEART of GOD. People with this gift regularly seek GOD'S presence through worship, fasting, prayer, and adherence to HIS principals. Known as the "Fear of the Lord," this gift maintains alignment with the Heart and Mind of GOD. If you align with HIS purpose, HE will talk to and operate through you more often.

21. **Intuitive Recognition & Compassion (Mercy):** This operation gift empowers you to deeply empathize and engage in compassionate acts for people suffering from physical, material, and emotional distress. Those with this gift demonstrate concern and kindness in situations often overlooked by others. This spiritual stream can be categorized by three functions: (1) highly sensitive to the feelings of others; (2) is sincere and authentic; and (3) demonstrates the highest forms of gentleness.

What to Take Away From This Section

You should now have a general understanding of the basic streams, functions, and channels of intuitive operation.

Key Points From Chapter 6

1. More than communication, GOD provides you with tangible power.
2. Revelation is often an invitation to power.
3. Spiritual gifts support the deployment of supernatural knowledge and power to influence the "gardens of the world tangibly."
4. The terms *Dimensional* and *Spiritual* refers to the function of operating in multiple realms and planes of existence, beyond the naturally seen, three-dimensional world.
5. The terms *Spiritual*, *Intuitive*, *Metaphysical* and, *Supernatural*, all have the same meaning.
6. Your Spirit contains all supernatural abilities required for you to prosper on Earth. Your Spirit is the epitome of who you are.
7. *Spiritual streams*, also known as *operation gifts* are supernatural abilities that flow continuously through your character traits. These gifts can be found in Romans 12.
8. Spiritual gifts are deployed intermittently to fulfill the purposes of GOD on a moment-by-moment basis. These gifts can be found in 1 Corinthians 12 and Isaiah 11.
9. In partnership with The Holy Spirit, your Spirit performs extraordinary exploits. These gifts are not natural but divine in function and operation.
10. There are 21 primary supernatural gifts given by GOD.

Chapter 7

Discerning The Revelatory Dimension

Identifying the Source of Intuitive Messages

Section 1: The Destination of Intuitive Messages

Navigating the Voices in Our Minds

Have you ever received a voice message from an unknown number, only to listen days later to find that the sender had important information for you? In a similar fashion, our minds and hearts often contain unopened messages sent to us by GOD. In previous chapters, you've learned that spiritual gifts such as the Gift of Prophecy (intuitive communication), are guided by The Holy Spirit to strengthen us in changing the lives of others. Now it's time to lay the framework for receiving supernatural messages.

GOD or not GOD is the question? With hundreds of thoughts running across our minds, how can we be sure we are hearing from GOD? As a leader in the Christian community, I have witnessed the release of many prophetic messages that did not corroborate with the heart of GOD. Unfortunately, in these occurrences, the recipient is often left confused, frustrated, or even angry when the messenger misses the target.

Therefore, without compromise, I would like to clearly state that every thought you receive is not inspired by GOD. **Through access granted from the Holy Spirit, the prophetic dimension is the spiritual plane that all of GOD'S spiritual gifts operate from.** GOD speaks through The Holy Spirit and HIS angels. As you will learn in the following sections, not all intuitive communication is originated from GOD's prophetic dimension.

Your Soul, Gatekeeper of Intuitive Messages

As mentioned in chapter 2, hearing and decoding intuitive messages from GOD requires that you receive intuitive prompts from outside of our three-dimensional world. This function involves communication from your multidimensional Spirit to your Soul. Remember, you are a Spirit living in a human Body with a Soul. You are not merely a human Body that possesses a Spirit. **You are an indestructible, multi-dimensional Spirit-being, living a three-dimensional experience through a human Body.**

While on Earth, your Soul plays the most crucial role in appropriately hearing from GOD.

For the purposes of free will, your Soul is the mediator between your Body and your Spirit. Your Soul makes the final decision regarding where your Body goes, what belief systems are embraced, and how you treat others. Contemplate this: **Your ears do not hear, your Soul does.** Your ears simply catch sounds waves and funnel them to your brain for processing.

Your Soul is responsible for establishing the standard operating procedures for your brain. Based upon past and present experiences and emotional state, your mind (a function of your Soul) processes information gathered from your eyes and ears. Accordingly, this is why you can say some- thing clearly, only for the intended party to misconstrue your words. Humans perceive with their Souls.

Your brain possesses functions exceeding the visible world. **Your brain is the hardware of your Soul, as it possesses the technological ability to capture invisible transmissions from multiple dimensions.** Correspondingly, the supernatural realm does not require human eyes or ears to communicate with your Soul's antenna (the brain). Like a projector, The Holy Spirit, angels, and evil spirits communicate through light, which is rendered to the "screen of your mind." This phenomenon is known as a "spiritual projection." Spiritual projections are recognized by the Soul as intuitive messages. It is your Soul's responsibility to govern information gathered from the unseen world.

Consequently, your Soul is bombarded with communications from this world and others. For those who can receive it, it was intended by GOD for your mind to be the birth canal of this reality. Anything seeking to exist in this realm must gain agreement from the Souls of humanity. Even Jesus needed to take human form to redeem mankind lawfully. Hopefully, you see how vital your Soul is and why it is so difficult for us to hear from GOD. I understand things may have become quite weighty. Consider re-reading chapter 2 The Mechanic of Human Intuitiveness, for further comprehension. For now, know that all intuitive messages are directed to your Soul.

What to Take Away From This Section

You should now understand that your Soul is the mediator of all intuitive functions, and through your free-will. GOD desires to develop your Soul into its original design.

Key Points From Section 1

1. Through access granted from the Holy Spirit, the prophetic dimension is the spiritual plane that all of GOD'S spiritual gifts operate from.
2. You are an indestructible, multidimensional Spirit-being, living a three-dimensional experience through a human Body.
3. For the purposes of free will, your Soul is the mediator between your Body and your Spirit.
4. Your ears do not hear, your Soul does, they simply catch sounds waves and funnel them to your brain for processing. Interpretation belongs to your Soul.
5. Your Soul is responsible for establishing the standard operating procedures for your brain.
6. Your brain is the hardware of your Soul, possessing the technological ability to capture invisible transmissions from multiple dimensions.
7. Spiritual projections occur when The Holy Spirit, angels, and evil spirits communicate to your Soul through light. Spiritual projections are recognized by the Soul as intuitive messages.

Section 2: Navigating the Realm of Intuitive Messages

Identifying 4 Sources of Intuitive Messages

The first and most important step we need to perform before decoding an intuitive message is to identify the source of the communication. But before we go any further, let's take a step forward in reconciling terms. **Intuitive messages can be derived from a variety of sources, prophetic messages are only derived by GOD through The Holy Spirit or His angels.** When the term *prophetic message* is used, the assumption is that it originated from GOD. **Prophetic messages carry the blueprint of creation in them.** Every time the Holy Spirit or an angel delivers a prophetic message, the fragrance of Heaven is released over your life. This statement calls for a deeper understanding that only comes through a relationship with GOD.

For further clarification, **prophetic messages can be classified as intuitive messages since they are delivered through the metaphysical realm, but all intuitive messages may not be from GOD; this would disqualify them from classification as prophetic messages.** If it is a GOD-given prophetic message, we are tasked with interpreting it, as further detailed in chapter 8. Though, if it is an intuitive message not offered by GOD, we need to manage or discard the communication appropriately. **Intuitive messages can be generated from four primary sources: GOD, Demonic Spirits, the Body, or the Soul.** Below is an overview of four primary sources of intuitive messages.

1. **GOD**: GOD is the first source of intuitive communication. Through delivery from the Holy Spirit, GOD communicates regarding the various circumstances surrounding our lives. More than merely intuitive, these are prophetic messages. Once validated, prophetic messages must be handled with extreme care. Let's

take a more in-depth look at how we can identify communications from GOD.

Why GOD Communicates:
a. To provide a sense of peace in times of trouble;
b. To restore trust in HIM;
c. To promote the growth of your Soul (mind, will, emotions and intellect);
d. To lead you into your perfect purpose;
e. To teach you how to live like Jesus; and
f. To shape the world around you.

How GOD Communicates:

a. By deploying the Holy Spirit and the angelic realm to project images and thoughts from Heaven to your Soul (mind, will, emotions and intellect);
b. By sending physical and emotional to your Body and Soul;
c. By releasing prophetic messages into the minds and mouths of others for your benefit; and
d. By visiting you in dreams (see process mentioned in point 'a' of this section) or inviting your Spirit to have a direct encounter him through a vision.

How to Identify Communication from GOD:

a. Experiencing sudden, unexplained peace during turbulent times;
b. Experiencing unexplained physical healing;
c. Experiencing sudden bursts of wisdom and knowledge when making decisions;
d. Experiencing a sudden burst of strength to complete tasks; and
e. Experiencing a sustained sense of purpose absent the world's embrace.

2. **Demonic Spirits**: Demonic entities are the second source of intuitive communication. At times, they can be the origin of dreams or nightmares, depression, or sickness. These are solely classified as intuitive messages. **Evil spirits supernaturally project images and thoughts to suppress our availability for use by GOD.** In other words, the demonic realm desires to prevent GOD using you to shape the gardens of the world. The Judeo-Christian bible makes hundreds of, often overlooked, references pertaining to "gates" and "doors." **Demonic spirits use interdimensional portals, commonly referred to as doors, to access human bodies and minds.** These "open doors" are often generated through an agreement with the demonic realm, in the form of unrepentant sins. For example: If someone perpetually lusts after others, the evil energy or sin created by the behavior can create an entryway for a demonic spirit of lust to access them. Consequently, the individual may experience sexual dreams meant to encourage them into relationships that would ultimately derail their future. In the Book of John 10:10, Jesus said that the enemy comes "only to steal and kill and destroy." We must be on high alert from communications originated from evil spirits. Let's take a deeper look at how we can identify the demonic realm's function of communication.

Why the Demonic Realm Communicates:

    a. To provoke fear in the areas of your personal domain;
    b. To extinguish your love for GOD;
    c. To stunt or regress the growth of your Soul;
    d. To mislead your from your purpose by sending intuitive messages that rob your time and emotional currency;

e. To present doubt in your ability to achieve prosperity (i.e., relationships, finance, supernatural ability, etc.); and
f. To condemn and accuse in hopes that you will never go to GOD for forgiveness, guidance, and restoration. Never let them isolate you. Jesus came, died, rose and ascended so that you would not live under condemnation.

How the Demonic Realm Communicates:

a. By projecting images and thoughts from their dimension to your Soul (mind, will, emotions and intellect) as outlined in 2 Corinthians 10, by Apostle Paul;
b. By sending pain and a variety of sickness to your Body;
c. By projecting thoughts and words into the minds and mouths of others to harm you; and
d. By visiting you in dreams through the process mentioned in point 'a' or engaging your Spirit and Soul in direct battle while you are asleep.

How to Identify Communication from Demonic Spirits:

a. Experiencing sudden, unexplained anxiety or fear while processing a thought;
b. Experiencing unexplained physical illness;
c. Experiencing unexplainable confusion when making decisions;
d. Experiencing a constant desire to isolate yourself; and
e. Experiencing anger or disappointment with GOD.

3. **The Body**: The Human Body is the third source of intuitive communication. When having a moment of

deep anxiousness, have you ever noticed you begin to experience discomfort in your stomach? What does your stomach have to do with the thoughts in your mind? The short answer, the Body communicates through intuitive messages. **Through the neurological and endocrine systems, the Body communicates signals to the brain.** Through a labyrinth of neurologically-transmitted chemical signals and hormones, your Body creates what is known at the "feedback loop." This involves communication moving from the brain, through various glands in the Body, returning back to the brain. This system encourages our emotional state, appetite, bodily growth, reproduction, and metabolism. **Keep in mind, the brain is a part of the Body. The brain is also the hardware for the Soul. Your Soul and Body were fascinatingly tied together."** I guess one could say you were reverently and marvelously designed. Nevertheless, **if we confuse emotional signals caused by our Body with the voice of GOD, we will be misled.** Let's take a more in-depth look at how we can identify the Body's functions of communication.

Why the Body Communicates:

a. to notify the Soul of a bodily malfunction, i.e., organ failing;
b. to prepare the mind for engagement, i.e., a strong bodily posture or movement can release hormones in the mind to be alert or relaxed; and
c. to notify the Soul of unrecognized emotional distress, i.e., shaking cause be extended periods of anxiousness.

How the Body Communicates:

a. by sending to information generated by the bodies nervous and endocrine systems to the Soul for processing, i.e., nightmares from eating bad food.

How to Identify Communication from the Body:

a. experiencing physical pains;
b. experiencing chronic fatigue;
c. experiencing malfunctions in bodily parts ;
d. experiencing abnormal growths in the Body (could be associated with suppressed emotions through the Body's feedback loop); and
e. experiencing hyperactivity (possibly from food or chemical imbalances).

4. **The Soul**: The Soul is the fourth source of intuitive communication. The Soul has the ability to generate its own thoughts and emotions. **Your Soul can only create intuitive messages, not prophetic messages. Confusing our thoughts for GOD'S will lead us to places of despair.** As a reminder, the Soul is comprised of our mind, will, emotions, and intellect. Stress, unresolved conflicts, loneliness, and other difficult situations can provoke intuitive messages that affect us by influencing our critical minds and emotions. For instance, rumors of your employer potentially laying people off may generate a season of "sub-conscious" anxiousness. During that period, you may be more apt to react in manners inconsistent with your character. **If the Soul receives and em- braces messages delivered to our Spirits by GOD, our mind, will, emotions, and intellect become supernatural. In this instance, intuitive messages transform into prophetic messages.** It is critical that we do not con fuse our thoughts with GOD'S. Let's look at how

we can identify the Soul's function and purpose of communication.

Why the Soul Communicates:

a. To protect the Body from danger;
b. To prevent emotional distress; and
c. To develop relationships with others.

How the Soul Communicates:

a. By self-processing information stored in the brain and generating responses such as good or bad, thoughts, emotions and dreams, i.e., generating depression from information in your sub-conscious;
b. By processing and reacting to data generated by the Body's nervous and endocrine systems, i.e., generating anxiety in response to chronic pain;
c. By accepting and breeding thoughts and ideas projected by the demonic realm; generating fits of rage as a result of a demonic projection; and
d. By accepting and breeding thoughts and ideas projected by GOD to your Spirit, i.e., generating bursts of faith to trust GOD through empowerment by The Holy Spirit.

How to Identify Communication from the Soul:

a. Experiencing thoughts that encourage emotional instability, i.e., emotion-led double-mindedness or indecisiveness;
b. Experiencing thoughts centered around self-preservation over others or GOD'S plan;
c. Experiencing thoughts that center on the way others perceive you i.e. making decisions for acceptance; and

d. Experiencing thoughts that reject extended processes of growing, learning or building.

Managing the 4 Sources of Intuitive Messages

As you have learned, the Human Body, Soul, and Spirit were interwoven by Heaven's multidimensional technology. We operate at an absolute deficit when diagnosing our feelings, sickness, or point of purpose through a one-dimensional scope. Through daily, Holy Spirit-led self-introspection, all intuitive messages must be appropriately managed or discarded. Accordingly, please embrace the following:

1. **Prophetic Messages from GOD:** must be honored, interpreted, recorded, and adhered to;
2. **Intuitive Messages from Demonic Spirits:** must be rejected and their interdimensional access points (doors) must be identified (sin in your life);
3. **Intuitive Messages from the Body:** must be investigated and requirements to adjust physical and emotional health should be adhered to; and
4. **Intuitive Messages from the Soul:** must be consistently monitored and managed through personal development along with prayer, fasting and active relationship with GOD.

It is not GOD'S desire for you to beat your Soul into submission. Instead, it is HIS purpose for your Spirit to partner with HIM in developing your mind, will, emotions, and intellect until you become the original version of yourself. Through intention, your Soul can become an expert mediator, seamlessly navigating intuitive messages. As you embrace this approach, you will reach the greatest heights of GOD'S Heart. Where you find GOD'S Heart, you will find HIS Voice and Hand. Because GOD **loved** the world, HE gave Jesus and all that comes with Him. Seek GOD's heart, and all of HIS gifts will follow.

What to Take Away From This Section

You should now understand that true prophetic messages originate from GOD while intuitive messages derive from our Souls, Bodies, or the Demonic dimension.

Key Points From Section 2

1. Intuitive messages can be derived from a variety of sources, prophetic messages are only derived by GOD through The Holy Spirit or His angels. When the term "prophetic message" is used, the assumption is it originated from GOD.
2. Prophetic messages can be classified as intuitive messages since they are delivered through the metaphysical realm, but all intuitive messages may not be from GOD, disqualifying them from being classified as prophetic messages.
3. Prophetic messages carry the blueprint of creation inside of them.
4. Intuitive messages can be generated from four primary sources GOD, Demonic Spirits, the Body, or the Soul.
5. GOD uses the Holy Spirit and the angelic realm to speak to your Spirit, which speaks to your Soul (mind, will, emotions, and intellect).
6. Demonic spirits use interdimensional portals, commonly referred to as doors, to access and speak to the Soul. These "open doors" are often generated through an agreement with the demonic realm, in the form of unrepentant sins.
7. The Human Body speaks to the Soul through the neurological and endocrine systems by a process known as the "feedback loop."
8. Your Soul can create its own intuitive messages. These are not prophetic messages. It is not GOD'S desire for you to "beat" your Soul unto submission, but partner with HIM in developing your mind, will, emotions, and intellect until you become the original version of yourself.

Section 3: Subconscious Intuitive Intervention

Embracing Dreams as Intuitive Messages

As mentioned in chapter 4, the Holy Spirit communicates through dreams. It is crucial to include dreams as a form of intuitive communication. In fact, dreams are often the most valued source of communication for many. GOD understands that while awake, you are likely focusing on tasks that you believe are required to support your livelihood. For most, it is difficult to listen to an unseen world, when our "very real" material world is consistently placing demands. **While asleep, your Body and Soul are in a state of rest; therefore, you are readily available to receive information with minimal conscious interruption.** Appropriately, I am sure that you can see why the vehicle of dreams is a common choice for GOD in communicating with mankind.

Throughout the Judeo-Christian Bible, GOD used dreams to communicate messages to humanity. Prior to learning the fundamentals of prophetic operation, it is essential to consider dreams as important prophetic messages. **Divinely inspired dreams are precious gifts from GOD.** Many of your dreams could be inspired by the Holy Spirit, delivered directly to you, from the heart and mind of GOD. **If you are not interpreting or recalling dreams given to you by GOD, you are likely evading critical information needed for you to navigate the winds of life.**

An excellent reference in the Judeo-Christian Bible supporting GOD's communication through dreams is found in Job33. The passage reads: *Why do you complain to HIM that HE responds to no one's words? For GOD does speak—now one way, now another—though no one perceives it. In a dream, in a vision of the night, when deep sleep falls on people as they slumber in their beds, he may speak in their ears and terrify them with warnings, to turn them from wrongdoing and keep them from pride, to preserve them from the pit, their lives from perishing by the sword.*

    The scripture above reveals that GOD is continually speaking to people throughout the day, yet HIS words are not understood. However, while sleeping, GOD is able to use those captive moments to talk to HIS people through the vehicle of dreams. Dreams and their interpretation are elusive. Everyone dreams. Yet, as our eyes open each morning, they quickly vanish. For those missing out on their dreams, I implore you to ask GOD to restore them to you. After doing this, pay close attention each morning for HIS answer and be sure to record the dream. As we begin unlocking the mysteries of decoding, consider GOD-given dreams to be prophetic messages.

What to Take Away From This Section

You should now understand the importance of receiving, interpreting, and embracing dreams as intuitive messages.

Key Points From Section 3

1. Dreams are a form of intuitive communication, they can become prophetic messages when inspired by guide.
2. When sleeping, your Body and Soul are in a state of rest; therefore, you are readily available to receive information with minimal conscious interruption.
3. Divinely inspired dreams are precious gifts from GOD containing critical information needed for you to navigate the winds of life.
4. If you forget your dreams, through prayer, ask GOD to reinstate the gift. Be sure to honor your dreams by recording them.

Chapter 8

Decoding The Revelatory Dimension

Interpreting Advanced Intuitive Messages

Section 1: The Source and Purpose of Prophetic Messages

The Source of Prophetic Interpretation

The Bible is filled with examples of prophetic message delivery, supernatural dreams, and their interpretation. The scriptures record that GOD often communicated through signs, miracles, symbols, word pictures, or symbols to convey hidden messages. These messages often required decoding to be understood.

Interpretation of intuitive messages absent The Holy Spirit creates opportunities for miscommunication with GOD. As we continue, remember intuitive messages can be generated by four sources. **The Holy Spirit is our ultimate guide on determining sources of intuitive communication, their meaning, and how to manage them.**

In Chapter 7, we focused on uncovering sources and purposes of intuitive communication based upon human feelings and reactions. This is a starting place, not a resting place. Our emotions and bodily reaction are unreliable compasses. Eventually, as one enters into a deeper relationship with GOD, in-depth and more detailed conversations are experienced. The Judeo-Christian Bible is filled with ordinary men and women who spoke of detailed future events that could have only been given by GOD. The best news, GOD never changes, and HE wants to share that same type of relationship with you.

Beyond secondary knowledge, advance prophetic people operate from a position of intimacy with GOD that allows them to know HIS language and desires. Throughout the next few sections, we will take steps in understanding and interpreting the language of GOD.

Interpreting the 5 Purposes of Prophetic Messages

One of the most common vehicles of prophetic messages from GOD is the revelatory vehicle of dreams. Many of the dreams recorded in the Judeo-Christian Bible often appear ridiculous. Yet, their interpretations are quite profound. Most importantly, the dreams had a purpose. Remember, **GOD speaks with intention and purpose. A purpose-driv- en life = hearing from GOD.** Likely, GOD's purpose for speaking involves the management of the domain given to you by GOD to develop and guard. **GOD will deliver prophetic messages for the purpose of warning, foretelling, counsel, encouragement, or impartation.** Let's take a closer look at the five purposes of prophetic messages:

1. **Warning: GOD sends prophetic warnings to notify us of potential dangers or unintended outcomes.** In chapter 2 of the Book of Matthew, Joseph received a prophetic message of the king's desire to kill his infant, Jesus Christ. Consequently, Joseph was able to move his family out of harm's way.
2. **Foretelling: GOD sends foretelling prophetic messages so we can predict or forecast future events.** In chapter 37 of the Book of Genesis, Joseph received a prophetic message about his brothers bowing down to him. During approximately 13 years of despair, Joseph could only hope that his dream would come to pass. Ultimately, it did, he became Egypt's second in command- saving his fellow Israelites from their famine afflicted land.
3. **Counsel: GOD sends prophetic messages of counsel to guide us in our decision-making.** According to the first two chapters of the Book of Matthew, Joseph considered divorcing Mary when he became aware of her supernatural pregnancy. GOD sent an angel carrying a prophetic message to convince Joseph that the pregnancy was of GOD.

4. **Encouragement: GOD sends prophetic messages of encouragement to give us hope and stimulate our minds to operate within our personal authority.** In the seventh chapter of the Book of Judges, the soldier Gideon received a prophetic message in the form of a dream that turned his hopelessness into absolute surety. Through GOD'S encouragement he went on to win against the opposing army.
5. **Impartation: GOD sends us prophetic messages of impartation carrying supernatural power, wisdom, and understanding to manage our personal domain.** In the third chapter of the 2 Kings, the Judeo-Christian Bible GOD appeared to Solomon in a dream. The dream resulted in GOD supernaturally giving Solomon unmatched wisdom and wealth.

This section should encourage you or someone you know in the long-awaited pursuit of answers from GOD. Today's generations are often alone as they make important life decisions. It is possible that the world is experiencing a mentorship epidemic. Nevertheless, a part of the "good news" is that GOD still speaks and has no intention of stopping.

What to Take Away From This Section

You should now understand the five general functions and purposes of prophetic messages.

Key Points From Section 1

1. Interpretation of intuitive messages absent The Holy Spirit creates opportunities for miscommunication with GOD.
2. The Holy Spirit is our ultimate guide on determining sources of intuitive communication, their meaning, and how to manage them.
3. Beyond secondary knowledge, advance prophetic people operate from a position of intimacy with GOD that allows them to know HIS language and desires.
4. GOD speaks with intention and purpose. A purpose-driven life = hearing from GOD.
5. GOD will deliver prophetic messages for the purpose of Warning, Foretelling, Counsel, Encouragement, or Impartation.
6. GOD sends prophetic Warnings to notify us of potential dangers or unintended outcomes.
7. GOD sends Foretelling prophetic messages so we can predict or forecast future events.
8. GOD sends prophetic messages of Counsel to guide us in our decision-making.
9. GOD sends prophetic messages of Encouragement to give us hope and stimulate our minds to operate within our personal authority.
10. GOD sends us prophetic messages of impartation carrying supernatural power, wisdom, and understanding to manage our personal domain.

Section 2: Interpreting the Structure of Prophetic Messages

Identifying 5 Structures of Prophetic Messages

Once we have identified the purpose of the prophetic message, our next objective is to determine its structure. **GOD structures prophetic messages as Literal, Parable, Reversal Repetition, or Progression form.** Let's take a closer look at the seven structures of prophetic messages.

1. **Literal** (objective): **GOD sends prophetic messages in literal form to encourage complete clarity during interpretation.** In this structure, the interpretation of symbolism is not required. Those possessing the gifts of Intermittent Governing Predication & Demand (The Office of the Prophet), Predication & Demand (The Gift of Prophecy), or Intuitive Information Reception (Word of Knowledge) are likely to receive literal-structured prophetic messages (refer to Chapter 6).

2. **Parable** (allegories and association): **GOD sends prophetic messages in parable form to protect the contents of the message.** Most prophetic messages, especially dreams, are parables by which objects, people, colors, numbers, and even one's actions are symbolic.

3. **Reversal** (replacing one person or thing with another): **GOD sends prophetic messages in reversal form to show us another person's state of being.** This frequently occurs in open-visions or dreams (read chapter 4). Through reversal, the prophetic operator becomes one of the symbols within the prophetic encounter by seeing through the eyes of another person.

4. **Repetition** (reoccurring): **GOD sends prophetic messages in repetition from to magnify the importance of the communication.** This structure

is common in open and closed visions and dreams. In the 41st chapter of Genesis in the Judeo-Christian Bible, Pharaoh received a dream twice (which holds prophetic symbolism), because GOD was going to bring the dream to pass.

5. **Progression** (various phases): **GOD sends prophetic messages in progression form to outline key focuses of the communication.** This structure is almost uniquely exclusive to dreams. In progression, you may have multiple dreams dealing with the same subject, as each successive dream dealing with a different aspect.

Being The Master Architect, GOD has a way of structuring prophetic messages from a variety of vantage points to enhance our ability to interpret HIS messages to us.

Structures are provided by GOD to encourage prophetic accuracy.

What to Take Away From This Section

You should now understand the five general structures of prophetic messages.

Key Points From Section 2

1. GOD structures prophetic messages as Literal, Parable, Reversal Repetition, or Progression form.
2. GOD sends prophetic messages in literal form to encourage complete clarity during interpretation.
3. GOD sends prophetic messages in parable form to protect the contents of the message.
4. GOD sends prophetic messages in reversal form to show us another person's state of being.
5. GOD sends prophetic messages in repetition form to magnify the importance of the communication.
6. GOD sends prophetic messages in progression form to outline key focuses of the communication.
7. Being The Master Architect, GOD has a way of structuring prophetic messages from a variety of vantage points to enhance our ability to interpret HIS messages to us.

Section 3: Interpreting Symbolism in Prophetic Messages

Interpreting 6 Common Symbols Found in Prophetic Messages

GOD speaks according to our level of cognition. In addition to biblical symbols, many prophetic messages contain figures that come from our present experience. When Jesus spoke in parables, He used symbols that were part of the everyday life of listeners over 2,000 years ago. Since many people in ancient Israel were familiar with farming, Jesus used activities such as plowing, sowing, planting, and reaping as metaphors for Heavenly Principals. Today, GOD utilizes the most appropriate symbols to speak to us in ways we can relate to.

Jesus often spoke in parables or symbolism to the unbelieving. In these cases, His intention was likely to lead them to humility by seeking GOD for understanding. While explaining His usage of parables, Jesus said, "Though seeing, they do not see; though hearing, they do not hear or understand. For this people's heart has become calloused, they hardly hear with their ears, and they have closed their eyes. Otherwise, they might see with their eyes, hear with their ears, understand with their hearts and turn, and I would heal them" (Matthew 13:13) **To properly interpret symbolism from GOD, you will need to seek the counsel of The Holy Spirit, through a moldable heart.**

There are millions of symbols that GOD uses to speak to us. It is nearly impossible to remember them all, without The Holy Spirit's leading. Accordingly, the Glossary of Common Signs and Symbols has been added as Appendix 'A' for your reference. However, it is important to remember the main categories of symbols. **GOD includes symbolism such as Numbers, Colors, People, Settings, Times and Season, and Objects in prophetic messages.** Let's take a closer look at the six fundamental symbols of prophetic messages.

1. **Numbers**: One of the most significant symbols of prophetic messages is the presentation of numbers. Identifying the purpose of numbers in a dream will provide the interpreter with critical points of application.
2. **Colors**: The identification of both extreme and subtle colors, as well as their patterns, are key to understanding the texture of a dream. Proper interpretation of colors supports understanding of whether the prophetic message is an announcement of something good or bad.
3. **People**: Just as in the case with other symbols, often, the people who appear in prophetic messages such as dreams are symbolic. At times, even the dreamer's role in the dream may be symbolic of something else.
4. **Settings**: Where is the storyline of the prophetic message taking place? In many dreams, the storyline transitions from one setting to another. These details are significant in discovering the meaning of prophetic messages.
5. **Times and Seasons:** Noting *WHEN* the prophetic message is referring, is as significant as where it takes place. Identifying the meaning behind times and seasons can reveal whether the prophetic message is referencing past, present, or future events.
6. **Objects:** Cars, elevators, bicycles, and other many other objects are often used by GOD to provide specificity to prophetic messages. Narrowing down the purpose of each object will provide the details necessary to receive GOD's special message clearly.

GOD speaks to us concerning our relationship with Him, our jobs, our health, and our relationships with others. Prophetic messages could reveal the future or provide counsel regarding urgent situations in our lives. A miscalculation in prophetic interpretation could lead to discouragement. **When a prophetic message is received, immediately**

write down all of the symbols and their placement, so that you do not lose critical points of GOD's intention.

What to Take Away From This Section

You should now understand the six categories of symbols GOD uses to add depth to prophetic messages.

Key Points From Section 3

1. To properly interpret symbolism from GOD, you will need to seek the counsel of The Holy Spirit, through a moldable heart.
2. GOD includes symbolism such as Numbers, Colors, People, Settings, Times and Season, and Objects in prophetic messages.
3. When a prophetic message is received, immediately write down all of the symbols and their placement, so that you do not lose critical points of GOD's intention.

Section 4: Interpreting the Proper Application of Prophetic Messages

Identifying the 4 Points of Application in Prophetic Messages

You have learned how to identify the source, purpose, structure, and symbols of prophetic messages. Now it's time to learn about how to apply them. The term "application" has two general definitions (1) a formal request to engage in an activity or (2) the act of placing something into operation. Let's combine the definitions as its related to the prophetic dimension. **"Prophetic application" is the process of gaining Heaven's approval of your interpretation, before placing a prophetic message into operation.** This process involves hearing and verifying crucial aspects of the GOD'S message to you or someone else.

Application is the final stage of prophetic interpretation. Prophetic application requires deeper prophetic function. **When interpreting prophetic messages, The Holy Spirit is likely to speak through four of the six intuitive prompts: Inner Witness, Remembrance, Hastening, or Leadings. Through His mentorship, you will decode the proper application of the prophetic message by decoding the Intended Party, Circumstance, Tense, and Instruction of prophetic messages.** Let's take a closer look at four main points of application in prophetic messages.

1. **Intended Party:** Who does the prophetic message refer to? Messages from GOD could be addressed to you, other people, groups, businesses, regions, nations, etc. You certainly do not want to deliver mail from GOD to the wrong address. This is the most critical point of prophetic application.
2. **Circumstance:** What Circumstance caused the prophetic message to be sent from Heaven? Through

the gifts of Intuitive Information Reception (Word of Knowledge) or Intermittent Prediction & Command (Gift of Prophecy), you can determine the past, present, or future events that trigger the release of the prophetic message. Prophetic messages are more potent when one is able to accurately articulate GOD'S response to a specific circumstance. Detailed messages bring deeper intimacy by reminding recipients that GOD never left them.

3. **Tense:** Is the prophetic message coming to pass in the past, present, future? In contrast to "circumstance" (centering on the person's life), the application of "tense" focuses on the outcomes of the prophetic message itself. When is GOD going to enforce the prophetic message?

4. **Instruction:** Does the prophetic message contain instructions for the recipient? Is there an act of faith required to release the provisions outlined in the prophetic message? Is a behavior modification needed to comply with a prophetic warning? If an instruction is not followed, the prophetic message will likely detach.

5. Right message, wrong predicted time? Right message, wrong person? In either instance, an adverse effect occurs when prophetic messages are suggested to occur outside of GOD'S timing and intended party. As you will learn in chapter 8, lack of instruction can cause the recipient (whether you or someone else) to miss the provisions of the prophetic messages. **The appropriate application of prophetic messages suggests spiritual maturity.** In many cases, when it comes to prophetic operation, intuitive people are led by the human Soul rather than their Holy Spirit guided human Spirit. Do not let the Soul's desire for human validation pressure you into expediting prophetic safeguards. In other words, **do not allow a mortal body to make supernatural decisions.**

What to Take Away From This Section

You should now understand the four points of application required for mature prophetic interpretation.

Key Points From Section 4

1. "Prophetic application" is the process of gaining Heaven's approval of your interpretation, before placing a prophetic message into operation.
2. When interpreting prophetic messages, The Holy Spirit is likely to speak through four of the six intuitive prompts: Inner Witness, Remembrance, Hastening, or Leadings.
3. Proper prophetic interpretation involves decoding the Intended Party, Circumstance, Tense, and Instruction of prophetic messages.
4. The appropriate application of prophetic messages suggests spiritual maturity.
5. Do not let the Soul's desire for social validation pressure you into expediting prophetic safeguards.
6. Do not allow a mortal body to make supernatural decisions.

Section 5: Deploying Safeguards for Prophetic Interpretation

Outlining the Five Steps of Prophetic Interpretation

Congratulations! You are now ready to begin interpreting prophetic messages. As a reminder, while interpreting, The Holy Spirit is likely to provide intuitive prompts in the form of an Inner Witness, Remembrance, Hastening, or Leadings (review chapter 4). Let's summarize the five steps of prophetic interpretation.

Step 1: Identify Source: Is the prophetic message from GOD, an Evil Spirit, the Body, or the Soul? Review chapter 4 and chapter 7, as necessary;

Step 2: Identify Purpose: Is the prophetic message a Warning, Foretelling, Counsel, Encouragement, or Impartation? Review section 1 of this chapter, as necessary;

Step 3: Identify Structure: Is the prophetic message a Literal, Parable, Reversal, Repetition, or Progression structure? Review section 2 of this chapter, as necessary;

Step 4: Identify Symbols: What Numbers, Colors, People, Settings, Times and Seasons, and Objects are included in the prophetic message? Utilize the Glossary of Common Signs and Symbols found Appendix 'A,' as necessary; and

Step 5: Identify Application: Confirm the Intended Party, Circumstance, Tense, and Instruction encoded in the prophetic message as outlined in section 4 of this chapter.

Deploying the Five Steps of Prophetic Interpretation

Let's follow the five-step prophetic interpretation process to uncover a well-known dream involving the patriarch Joseph and Egypt's leader (Pharaoh) found in Book of Genesis 41:

When two full years had passed, Pharaoh had a dream: He was standing by the Nile, when out of the river there came up seven cows, sleek and fat, and they grazed among the reeds. After them, seven other cows, ugly and gaunt, came up out of the Nile and stood beside those on the riverbank. And the cows that were ugly and gaunt ate up the seven sleek, fat cows. Then Pharaoh woke up. He fell asleep again and had a second dream: Seven heads of grain, healthy and good, were growing on a single stalk. After them, seven other heads of grain sprouted—thin and scorched by the east wind. The thin heads of grain swallowed up the seven healthy, full heads. Then Pharaoh woke up; it had been a dream. In the morning, his mind was troubled, so he sent for all the magicians and wise men of Egypt. Pharaoh told them his dreams, but no one could interpret them for him. (Genesis 41:1-8)

"It is just as I said to Pharaoh: God has shown Pharaoh what he is about to do. Seven years of great abundance are coming throughout the land of Egypt, but seven years of famine will follow them. Then all the abundance in Egypt will be forgotten, and the famine will ravage the land. The abundance in the land will not be remembered, because the famine that follows it will be so severe. The reason the dream was given to Pharaoh in two forms is that the matter has been firmly decided by God, and God will do it soon. "And now let Pharaoh look for a discerning and wise man and put him in charge of the land of Egypt. Let Pharaoh appoint commissioners over the land to take a fifth of the harvest of Egypt during the seven years of abundance. They should collect all the food of these good years that are coming and store up the grain under the authority of Pharaoh, to be kept in the cities for food. This food should be held in reserve for the country, to be used during the seven years of famine that will come upon Egypt, so that the country may not be ruined by the famine." (Genesis 41:28-36)

(Be sure to read all 56 verses of Genesis 41)

Step 1: Identify Source- Is the prophetic message from GOD, an Evil Spirit, the Body, or the Soul? The prophetic message was delivered by GOD.

Step 2: Identify Purpose- Is the prophetic message a Warning, Foretelling, Counsel, Encouragement, or Impartation? The dream was purposed as a Foretelling prophetic message regarding a fourteen year period of Egypt's harvest. It was not a Warning since there was no action Pharaoh could have taken to avoid the famine. In verses 25 and 28 of the scripture, the prophetic operator, Joseph, reiterates to Pharaoh that GOD speaks regarding "what he is about to do."

Step 3: Identify Structure- Is the prophetic message Literal, Parable, Reversal, Repetition, or Progression structure? The prophetic message is: (1) a Parable because its riddled with symbolism that must be interpreted, and (2) according to Joseph (verse 32), it is also Repetition because Pharaoh had two dreams regarding the same matter.

Step 4: Identify Symbols- What Numbers, Colors, People, Settings, Times and Seasons, and Objects are included in the prophetic message? Some of the symbols of the prophetic message include: (1) the Nile River represents the economic life-stream of Egypt; (2) the number 7 represents GOD'S perfection; and (3) cows milk represents the sustainment of life).

Step 5: Identify Application- Confirm the Intended Party, Circumstance, Tense and Instruction encoded in the prophetic message. The Intended Party (Egypt), Circumstance (the economic power of Egypt and GOD'S ultimate rulership over it), Tense (the message was going to take place in the future), Instruction (Joseph told Pharaoh how to prepare for the seven year famine.)

Summarizing Interpretation: According to the scripture, Joseph interpreted that GOD was warning Pharaoh of what HE was about to do to Egypt. That there would be seven years of great abundance, but seven years of famine will follow them. To prepare him, GOD instructed Pharaoh to appoint commissioners to manage and save the grain during the seven years of abundance in preparation for the seven years of famine.

Though a dream was used as an example, remember, prophetic messages are received from GOD while you are awake and asleep. In either case, you should not deviate from the process of interpretation should. **It is often simpler to receive and recall detailed prophetic messages in the form of dreams because your conscious mind is not in contention with your Spirit. Through union with the Holy Spirit and the consistent deployment of personal authority, you will attain meticulous prophetic messages in your waken hours.**

What to Take Away From This Section

You should now understand how to apply all five steps of mature prophetic interpretation.

Key Points From Section 5

1. The five steps to interpret prophetic messages include identifying the Source, Purpose, Structure, Symbols, and Application.
2. It is often simpler to receive and recall detailed prophetic messages in the form of dreams because while asleep, your conscious mind is not in contention with your Spirit.
3. Through union with the Holy Spirit and the consistent deployment of personal authority, you will attain meticulous prophetic messages in your waken hours.

Chapter 9

Releasing The Revelatory Dimension

Safeguarding and Delivering
Prophetic Messages

Section 1: Delivering Prophetic Messages

Leveraging the Dimension of Faith

In the last chapter, you learned principles for interpreting the language of GOD. Now you will learn the framework for positively impacting others through your prophetic gift. Just know this, at times, you will miss the target. It is safe to say that no one likes to be mistaken, especially when an audience is involved. The fear of being mistaken often discourages people from delivering detailed prophetic messages. **Do not let your fear of embarrassment supersede your desire to be a Heavenly vessel.**

To operate in the supernatural, you must be bold in your relationship with GOD. Over the last 20 years, I have noticed that most prophetic messages lack essential details. **Ambiguous prophetic messages increase the potential loss of heavenly treasures.**

Absent specific information, it is difficult to identify when or if the prophetic message has been fulfilled. When recipients become aware of a prophetic message's validity, their faith is restored, and GOD is honored.

Prophetic operation is supernatural, and so are we. It requires our Soul to cede to our GOD-inspired Spirit. **Prophetic operation and accuracy are achieved through the supernatural "dimension of faith." Faith is the bridge between Heaven and Earth.**

Faith requires your Soul to have moments of doubt, leaving room for the Holy Spirit to partner with you. You do the natural, and He does the supernatural. In the Book of Hebrews the Apostle Paul stated: "without faith, it is impossible to please GOD." (Hebrews 11:6)

If we knew everything about the future, there would be no opportunity for the faith. Faith requires mystery. **Your Measure of Faith increases according to the measure of mystery you walk through daily** (revisit chapter 6). Exercises of faith in GOD act as demonstrations of your free-will to love HIM. Our time on Earth provides us the opportunity to give GOD something we will not be able to offer HIM in Heaven-blind love. The demonstration of this true love is why we are elevated to join HIM in eternity.

Six Stages of Managing Effective Prophetic Message Delivery

Heavenly Postal Service (HPS)

The prophetic delivery process can be likened to an intricate supply chain. When the prophetic message is received, the messenger applies the five-step interpretation process (revisit chapter 8), then decides how to frame the message, and deliver it. Then the person or group receiving the message interprets its meaning and chooses to accept or reject the message.

In 2015, I developed the Heavenly Postal Service (HPS) prophetic delivery system as a personal guide. Let's review the six-stages of the HPS system and why it's vital to the receipt, process- ing, and delivery of prophetic messages.

Stage 1 Package Received (Prophetic Message Received By Messenger): At this stage, the prophetic message has been received by the prophetic operator (you). The Holy Spirit often delivers packages as an intuitive picture, scripture, word, feeling, or dream. Like a fingerprint, GOD'S way of speaking to and through you will be unique. He acclimates intuitive prompts (messages or revelation we receive) to our distinct personalities, learning styles, intuitive abilities, and social norms. Throughout the Judeo-Christian Bible, GOD'S servants are recorded as having received revelation from Heaven in a countless variety of ways. In all accounts, GOD finds a way to deliver messages through those who are willing. **To be consistently chosen for prophetic package delivery, you must embrace a lifestyle of scanning your**

surroundings. Everywhere you go, make a habit of asking the Holy Spirit if there is anyone that He wishes to encounter.

Stage 2 Package Interpreted (Prophetic Message Assessed by Messenger): At this stage, the message is being interpreted by the prophetic operator. Though there is one step that must be completed before beginning the interpretation process, **assess the condition of your heart.** Remember, our Soul is the mediator of all intuitive messages. **The state of your Soul will likely determine whether or how you interpret and deliver the prophetic message.** Once the "heart-check" is complete, begin the prophetic interpretation process found in chapter 8.

Stage 3 Package Delivered (Prophetic Message Distributed to Recipient): At this stage, the prophetic operator is deploying the prophetic message to the recipient. When GOD releases a prophetic message, HE will provide instructions on the method of delivery.

Mature prophetic operators seek and act on the instructions received. Your package delivery is marked by the method you choose to express the message. Examples of prophetic message delivery include speaking, exclaiming, joking, singing, writing, or symbolic acts. **Improper delivery could nullify the validity of the prophetic message in Heaven.** Additionally, timing and the setting place a role in the successful delivery of the message. Prophetic messengers are not accountable for the success or failure of messages, only their precise interpretation, and delivery.

Stage 4 Package Received (Prophetic Message Received by Recipient): At this stage, the recipient's Soul is determining if the package is theirs and if they wish to open it or not. Remember, The Holy Spirit is responsible for guarding His word. He is an expert at ensuring that His messages get to those who need to hear it. He can achieve this in a multitude of ways. If a prophetic message is pure and clear, He will get it to those who need to hear it, when the time is right.

Stage 5 Package Interpreted (Prophetic Message Assessed by Recipient): At this stage, the recipient is interpreting the opened prophetic package. They are listening to the message in the light of their past experiences, present needs, and desire for the future, as well as their unique perspective on GOD'S Word and character. In a perfect situation, both the prophetic operator and the recipient yielded to the Holy Spirit, and through matured gifts, the prophetic message gained potency during the process.

Stage 6 Package Decisioned (Prophetic Message Processed by Recipient): At this stage, the recipient has discarded or walked away with the package. If the instruction was given-but not followed- the failure of "application" will cause the prophetic message to detach. Once you have delivered the message, it is the recipient's free-will that guides them as to whether or not they will respond. If the instruction wasn't given- but should have been- the recipient is responsible for interpreting and abiding by the conditions of the prophetic message.

By understanding our role in the prophetic delivery method, we delineate between our responsibility and that of the recipient. The process helps us to grow in prophetic wisdom and intuitive sensitivity, not only to GOD but in understanding the communication needs of those we are delivering to. Breaking the prophetic process into six simple parts demystifies prophecy to someone who is starting, by concentrating on one area at a time. If we discover a weakness in one area of the process, we can narrow our developmental focus.

What to Take Away From This Section

You should now understand the functions and importance of the six-stage prophetic delivery process.

Key Points From Section 1

1. Do not let your fear of embarrassment supersede your desire to be a Heavenly vessel.
2. Ambiguous prophetic messages increase the potential loss of heavenly treasures.
3. Prophetic operation and accuracy are only achieved through the supernatural "dimension of faith."
4. Faith is the bridge between Heaven and Earth.
5. Your Measure of Faith increases according to the measure of mystery you walk through on a daily basis.
6. Exercises of faith in GOD act as demonstrations of your free-will to love HIM.
7. Our time on Earth provides us the opportunity to give GOD something we will not be able to give HIM in Heaven, blind love.
8. There are six distinct stages to the delivery of prophetic messages.
9. To be consistently chosen for prophetic package delivery, you must embrace a lifestyle of scanning your surroundings.
10. Assess the condition of your heart before beginning the prophetic interpretation process. The state of your Soul will likely determine how you interpret and deliver the prophetic message.
11. When GOD releases a prophetic message, HE will provide instruction on the method of delivery. Mature prophetic operators seek and act on the instructions received.
12. Improper delivery could nullify the validity of the prophetic message in Heaven.

Section 2: 10 Intuitive Channels

Specified Content for Prophetic Messages

Now that you have learned about the methods of prophetic interpretation and delivery, it is time to put your gift into operation. But where? To answer this question, we must revisit the terms "personal authority" and "personal domain" found in Chapter 3. GOD provided you with the gifting and ability to partner with HIM in fulfilling your purpose on Earth. Domain refers to a region, realm, or territory. **Your personal domain is the specific sphere of influence or territory given to you by GOD. Personal authority is the gifting and supernatural ability given to you by GOD to protect and develop your personal domain.**

Your personal domain includes your family, your job or business, your Body, and your Soul- among many other areas. **GOD communicates with people on exercising personal authority over their personal domain.** Put another way, GOD speaks to you based upon your level and type of responsibility on Earth. Whether you are in government, ministry, business, a stay-at-home parent, or somewhere in between, GOD has a specific form of communication stream that HE uses to speak to you and others that speak your language.

The term "prophetic channel" refers to the stream that GOD uses to transmit specific "content" to a specific group of people. When you turn on your television, you pick up the remote and search for specified content based on channels. There are unique channels for those who are in business, love home improvement and speak a foreign language. Similarly, each prophetic channel delivers specified content across a variety of groups who share similar areas of personal authority. By segmenting content by groups, GOD can broadcast the same general message, to achieve cooperation and impact through HIS people all over the world.

Through GOD'S prophetic channels, business people strategically navigate market conditions, government leaders establish humanity-saving policies, and spiritual leaders gain supernatural insight and power to guide HIS people into protection and provision. In every case, their job is to connect to the appropriate channel to gain insight and power for impacting the landscape GOD has given then.

For clarity, GOD determines the prophetic channel(s) that you can have access to based upon your giftings and purpose on the Earth. Your job is to determine which channels you've been granted admission to. Let's review a handful of the many channels available in the prophetic dimension.

1. **The Prophetic Dimension (Spirit of Prophesy):** This prophetic channel provides "basic" content for receiving, interpreting, delivering, and operating within prophetic messages. As foretold by Jesus in Mark 16, this channel is available to all "who believe." In other words, every believer in Jesus has access to this channel through The Holy Spirit. GOD will speak to you regarding every area of your personal domain. The following channels are more "content focused." You may also have access to one or more prophetic channels.

2. **Prophetic Dimension Governance (Prophetic Presbytery):** This channel provides content for identifying GOD's purpose, providing spiritual impartations, and activating, and releasing people into their destiny. The group that receives this channel is typically comprised of spiritual leaders with established prophetic gifts, such as those of the prophetic office. Members of this channel engage in deep prophetic operations to prepare others for various seasons of their lives.

Common supernatural gifts associated: Word of Knowledge, Word of Wisdom, Intercessory Prayer, Proclaiming, Gift of Prophecy, Discernment, Healings, Counsel, Understanding, Reverence for GOD, and Leadership.

3. **Prophetic Evangelism:** This channel provides content for releasing the tangible Power of GOD to demonstrate the message of Jesus to those beyond the walls of the church. The groups that receive this channel vary, considering that it is the responsibility of all believers to declare the gospel of Christ. People who receive this channel have the ability to heal the sick and provide prophetic words in non-church environments. Prophetic evangelism is a powerful channel for any believer wanting to share the message of salvation in Jesus Christ with the world.

Common supernatural gifts associated: Word of Knowledge, Proclaiming, Gift of Prophecy, Mercy, Serving, Faith, Might, Discernment, Healings, and Miracles.

4. **The Marketplace:** This channel provides content for releasing the knowledge, wisdom, and understanding of GOD to impact economic spheres. The group that receives this channel is typically comprised of entrepreneurs occupying industries such as healthcare, education, entertainment, finance, and various forms of commerce. Those called to the marketplace by GOD are responsible for establishing economic vehicles that advance the will and heart of GOD.

Common supernatural gifts associated: Word of Wisdom, Proclaiming, Gift of Prophecy, Discernment, Giving, Teaching, Counsel, Faith, Understanding, and Leadership.

5. **The Government:** This channel provides streams for releasing the knowledge, wisdom, and understanding of GOD to impact the spheres of government. The group that receives this channel is typically comprised of spiritual, community, and political leaders who are accountable for building and maintain communities.

Common supernatural gifts associated: Word of Wisdom, Proclaiming, Gift of Prophecy, Discernment, Teaching, Mercy, Serving, Counsel, Understanding, and Leadership.

6. **Prophetic Counseling (Inner Healing/Deliverance):** This channel provides content for identifying and supernaturally incapacitating demonic influences that internally afflict humankind. The group that receives this channel is typically comprised of Believers in Christ that have an intuitive ability to bring a deep level of understanding, counsel, and prayer intervention to liberate people from negative emotional and spiritual hold. Members of this channel employ deep intuitive insight and spiritual authority to prepare others to enter into new seasons of their lives.

Common supernatural gifts associated: Word of Knowledge, Word of Wisdom, Intercessory Prayer, Proclaiming, Gift of Prophecy, Discernment, Healings, Counsel, Understanding, and Reverence for GOD.

7. **Prophetic Prayer:** This channel provides content for identifying the will of GOD and speaking HIS desires into existence through the form of prayer. Members of this channel are often awakened in the middle of the night, or early in the morning with a strong sense to pray. Although often overlooked, followers of Jesus can attain and operate in this gift.

Common supernatural gifts associated: Word of Knowledge, Intercessory Prayer, Proclaiming, Gift of Prophecy, Discernment, Healings, Might, Faith, Understanding, Interpretation of Tongues, and Reverence for GOD.

8. **Prophetic Vision (Seer Realm):** This channel provides members with a visual perception of the past, present, and future. Members of this channel often see activity in another dimension that others cannot.

Common supernatural gifts associated: Word of Knowledge, Intercessory Prayer, Proclaiming, Discernment, Understanding, and Reverence for GOD.

9. **Prophetic Worship:** This channel provides members with a real-time perception of the heart of GOD to be expressed on the Earth through spontaneous worship.

Members of this channel can release a dimension that draws others closer to GOD.

Common supernatural gifts associated: Word of Knowledge, Intercessory Prayer, Gift of Prophecy, Discernment, Healings, Faith, Understanding, Interpretation of Tongues, and Reverence for GOD.

10. **Prophetic Teaching:** This channel provides content for instructing others on the intention and original design of GOD. Members of this channel have a unique gift to teach the context of scripture, biblical prophecy and how to navigate various live events.

Common supernatural gifts associated: Word of Wisdom, Proclaiming, Counsel, Gift of Prophecy, Understanding, and Reverence for GOD.

GOD assigns you to the appropriate prophetic channel needed to collaborate with others. Your operation and spiritual gifts uniquely align with the ten channels outlined above. Your supernatural gifts (revisit chapter 6) represent your abilities, while your channels represent the various groups that you are apart.

What to Take Away From This Section

You should now understand the functions and importance of the six-stage prophetic delivery process.

Key Points From Section 2

1. Your personal domain is the specific sphere of influence or territory given to you by GOD. Personal authority is the gifting and supernatural ability given to you by GOD to protect and develop your personal domain.
2. GOD communicates with people on exercising personal authority over their personal domain.
3. The term "prophetic channel" refers to the stream that GOD uses to transmit specific "content" to a specific group of people.
4. The 10 basic prophetic channels are: The Prophetic Dimension, Prophetic Dimension Governance, Prophetic Evangelism, The Marketplace, The Government, Prophetic Counseling, Prophetic Prayer, Prophetic Vision, Prophetic Worship, and Prophetic Teaching.

Final Section: Closing Remarks

Success Through Collaboration and Deployment

This book was written to develop your ability to hear GOD through gaining an understanding of your naturally supernatural human composition, GOD's nature, and the functions of intuitive operation. Secondarily, the foundation was inserted for readers to begin delivering basic prophetic messages. The principles found in this book take time and intention to embrace. However, through leveraging the dimensions of faith, you will be surprised by GOD'S ability to use you. Remember, you were sent the universe's best Teacher to guide you back to your original design.

The lives of Jesus' disciples are the best case study as they demonstrate The Holy Spirit's ability to guide ordinary people into extraordinary feats. Once scared, abrasive, and reliant upon their basic-human understanding, they became bold, powerful, and full of the knowledge of GOD. They sought Jesus and came into advanced, intuitive function by identifying, employing, and unifying their personal authority. I have witnessed this very same shift among today's followers of Jesus. If you follow the three steps of activating your personal authority, you too will be delivered from fright to boldness, doubt to faith, and from confusion to maturity.

Finally, remember that personal authority is interrelated. Humanity was designed to be an orchestra, not a solo performance. GOD strategically melded others with gifts that complement and enhance yours. Embrace seasoned, character-tested spiritual leaders who can provide a platform to develop and immediately deploy your personal authority to impact the lives of others. Embrace those who can use your mentorship and be faithful to their development. GOD doesn't help those who help themselves, as much as HE helps those who help others.

References

1. Derek Kidner, Genesis, An Introduction and Commentary, Inter-Varsity Press.
2. Merrill F. Unger, Unger's Commentary on the Old Testament, Vol. I.
3. Dr. Myles Munroe, The Purpose and Power of Authority.
4. Allen Ross, The Bible Knowledge Commentary, Old Testament.
5. Warren Wiersbe, Be Loyal, Victor Books.
6. Dr. Paula Price, The Prophet's Handbook: A Guide to Prophecy and its Operation.
7. Gerald L. Schroeder, The Science of GOD: The Convergence of Scientific and Biblical Wisdom.
8. J. Dwight Pentecost, The Words and Works of Jesus Christ, Zondervan.
9. James Hope Moulton and George Milligan, The Vocabulary of the Greek Testament.
10. James Strong, The Exhaustive Concordance of The Bible.

About the Author

Forbes Finance Council member, U.S. Naval veteran, spiritual leader, and community organizer, Dr. Jason Jackson is a sought-after innovative theorist and transformational guide. Regularly covered by over 150 media outlets such as CNBC, TBN, and the Boston Globe, Dr. Jackson has earned a distinguished reputation as a social and economic pioneer. He is a devoted husband to his wife, Natalie, and father to his four children.

Dr. Jackson is internationally known for his position as the Founder and Chief Investment Officer of leading Investment Bank, where he is responsible for oversight of the firm's investment portfolio. He is frequently called upon by his peers to serve as an expert speaker in national conferences for the Association of Corporate Growth, Crittenden Real Estate Finance, and Noble Capital Markets.

In addition to his business initiatives, Dr. Jackson has established a broad array of community-centric platforms, ranging from food salvage to youth risk reduction programs. Through his leadership mobilization organization, Jackson Global Initiative, he serves as an advisor to government, community, and spiritual leaders and a diverse group of entrepreneurs. He has served on the board of over 30 diverse companies and committees. He currently serves as the Overseer and Senior Pastor of the Lion's Den Mission Base, located in Fort Lauderdale, Florida.

To contact the author please visit:
www.jacksonglobalinitiative.com
www.facebook.com/apjasonjackson/
Email: Administration@UNCPA.us

Appendix 'A'
Quick Reference Guides

32 Functions of The Holy Spirt

1) Provides Access to GOD-Eph. 2:18
2) Establishes Personal-authority-Luke 4:18
3) Provides Assurance-Gal. 4:6
4) Authors Scripture-2 Pet. 1:20-21
5) Baptizes-1 Cor. 12:13-14
6) Establishes Salvation-John 3:3-6
7) Commissions Assignments-Acts 13:24
8) Cleanses Souls-1 Thess. 3:13
9) Convicts of Wrongdoing-John 16:9
10) Creates-Gen. 1:2
11) Empowers-1 Thess. 1:5
12) Communes With Human Spirits-Acts 4:29
13) Gives Supernatural Ability-I Cor. 12:8
14) Authenticates Jesus-John 16:14
15) Guides in Truth-John 16:13
16) Helps in Times of Weakness-Rom. 8:26
17) Inspires Prayer-Eph. 6:18
18) Intervenes -Rom. 8:26
19) Interprets-1 Cor. 2:1
20) Leads-Rom. 8:14
21) Liberates-Rom. 8:2
22) Molds Morality-Gal. 5:18
23) Produces Character-Gal. 5:22
24) Empowers Believers-Luke 24:49
25) Stops Eternal Death-Rom. 8:11
26) Regenerates-Titus 3:5
27) Renews Souls -Rom. 15:16
28) Seals Salvation-Eph. 1:13
29) Strengthens-Eph. 3:16
30) Teaches-John 14:26
31) Testifies of Jesus-John 15:26
32) Leads Intimacy w/GOD-Phil. 3:3

Four Dimensions of Relationship With The Holy Spirit

He Dwells With You (First-Dimension): This relationship level with the Holy Spirit is experienced by those who have not yet decided to follow Jesus. The Holy Spirit walks beside them, encouraging the pursuit of their true identity in relationship with their Creator

He Lives In You (Second-Dimension): This relationship level occurs when The Holy Spirit lives in a person through the gift of salvation, and they are empowered to shape their Souls into the Character of GOD.

He Rests Upon You (Third-Dimension): This relationship level occurs when The Holy activates your intuitive abilities and supernatural gifts to impact others.

He Lives Through You (Fourth-Dimension): This relationship level occurs when The Holy Spirit can operate through you 24-hours a day, through full agreement from your Soul.

The 6 Major Intuitive Prompts From The Holy Spirit

Intuitive-Confirmation (Inner-Witness): Occurs when The Holy Spirit provides us with a strong affirmation (witness) of something going on in your life. Some refer to an inner witness as a "gut feeling." You are at peace in your decision, without understanding why.

Intuitive-Recollection (Remembrance): Occurs when The Holy Spirit instantaneously reminds you of a conversation, circumstance, or "learned knowledge" at a time you need it most.

Intuitive-Prompting (Hastening): Occurs when The Holy Spirit rapidly projects intuitive images or sounds towards you at a speed that requires your attention.

Intuitive-Guidance (Leadings): Occurs when The Holy Spirit fixates your attention away from or towards a specific area.

Dimensional-Perceptions (Visions): Occurs when The Holy Spirit enters you into a "deep state" to witness detailed visualizations of past, present, or future events.

Subconscious-Intervention (Dreams): Occurs when The Holy Spirit delivers messages while our Soul is in a state of rest.

7 Assignments For Intuitive Communicators

Declaring the Heart and Will of GOD
Identifying the Intuitive Nature of Others
Interpreting Messages from GOD
Encouraging the Discouraged
Providing Sound Counsel and Instruction
Comforting Those in Need
Demonstrating Morality to the World

5 Steps Prophetic Interpretation

Step 1: Identify Source- GOD, Evil Spirit, the Body, or the Soul as outlined in Chapter 4 and Chapter 7.

Step 2: Identify Purpose- Warning, Foretelling, Counsel, Encouragement, or Impartation, as outlined in Section 1 of Chapter 8.

Step 3: Identify Structure- Literal, Parable, Reversal, Repetition, or Progression structure, as outlined in Section 2 of Chapter 8.

Step 4: Identify Symbols- Numbers, Colors, People, Settings, Times and Seasons, and Objects as outlined in Section 3 of Chapter 8. Utilize the Glossary of Common Signs and Symbols found Appendix 'B,' as necessary.

Step 5: Identify Application- Confirm the Intended Party, Circumstance, Tense, and Instruction, as outlined in Section 4 of Chapter 8.

Six Stages of Managing Effective Prophetic Message Delivery Heavenly Postal Service (HPS)

Stage 1 Package Received (Prophetic Message Received By Messenger): At this stage, the prophetic message has been received by the prophetic operator (you).

Stage 2 Package Interpreted (Prophetic Message Assessed by Messenger): At this stage, the message is being interpreted by the prophetic operator (you).

Stage 3 Package Delivered (Prophetic Message Distributed to Recipient): At this stage, the prophetic operator is deploying the prophetic message to the recipient.

Stage 4 Package Received (Prophetic Message Received by Recipient): At this stage, the recipient's Soul is determining if the package is theirs and if they wish to open it or not.

Stage 5 Package Interpreted (Prophetic Message Assessed by Recipient): At this stage, the recipient is interpreting the opened prophetic package.

Stage 6 Package Decisioned (Prophetic Message Processed by Recipient): At this stage, the recipient has discarded or walked away with the package.

Appendix 'B'

Glossary of Common Signs and Symbols

Note: The following list is not meant to be exhaustive and cannot encompass all possible interpretations or appropriate applications outside of a prophetic message. There are millions of symbols that GOD uses to speak to us. It is nearly impossible to remember them all, without The Holy Spirit's leading.

However, it is important to remember the main categories of symbols. GOD includes symbolism such as Numbers, Colors, People, Settings, Times and Season, and Objects in prophetic messages. To accurately interpret symbolism from GOD, you will need to seek the counsel of The Holy Spirit, through a moldable heart. Try not to interpret symbols outside of the five-steps of interpretation outlined in chapter 8.

Blueprint for Hearing GOD

ONE:
Beginning Genesis 1:1
Father, Son, Holy Spirit 1 John 5:7
Unity John 17:21
First, New, Beginning Deut 6:4

TWO:
Witness, witnessing Matthew 18:16
Division, Separation 1 Tim 5:19
Hebrews 4:12
Discern
Confirmation

THREE:
Complete, Perfection, Witness, Godhead, Conform 1 John 5:6-7
Divine Perfection (Matthew 28:19)
Spirit, Soul, Body Yesterday, Today, tomorrow Witness 1 Timothy 5:19

FOUR:
Creation
Earth, Air, Fire Water- Four Elements
North, East, South, West- Four Directions
Spring, Summer, Fall, Winter- Four Seasons
Morning, Noon, Evening, Midnight- Four divisions of the day
World, Creative Work Ez 37:9
Four Rivers flow out of Eden Gen 2:10-14 Four Faces of The Cherubim

FIVE:
Grace Luke 9:16
Atonement
Five fold Ministry Eph 4:11
Service, Bondage Isaiah 1:12-14

SIX:
Number of man
Satan, flesh, carnal Rev. 13:18
Earth created for man in 6 days
Man created on the 6th day
Man without God
Flesh nature Numbers 11:20-21
Works of man Ex 20:9, 10

SEVEN:
Spiritual Perfection
Completion, Finished work, Rest (Genesis 2:1-3)
Completeness (Rev 1:12)
Ultimate Victory, Possession
Rev 11:15 1Kings 18:43
Labor for 7 years for bride

EIGHT:
New Beginnings
Eight souls saved in the flood
Number of Salvation 1 Peter 3:20 Liberty in Spirit
Separation unto God Exodus 22:30 Dying to self

NINE:
Judgement
Short of coming into Gods Divine Order Falling short
Finality Matt 15:33,34
9 Fruits of the Spirit
9 Gifts of the Spirit
Darkness, separation Matt 27:45, 46

TEN:
Perfection of Divine Order
Government Rev 2:10
Law, Order, Covenant Deu 4:13
Tithe, Measure
Trial, Testing
10   Commandments
10   Plagues in Egypt

ELEVEN:
End, Finish, Final
Incomplete, disorder,
lawlessness Genesis 27:9

Confusion, betrayal
11 apostles after Judas was
removed

TWELVE:
Perfection Of Government
12 Patriarchs
12 Apostles
12 Tribes of Israel
The Church, People of God
Discipleship, united, oversight
Gen 49:28 Church, discipleship
Matt 10:1-6

THIRTEEN:
Satan
Rebellion
Israel rebelled against God 13
times in Wilderness
Rejection
Backsliding Gen 14:4

FOURTEEN:
Deliverance
Salvation
Passover Exodus 12:6
Recreate, Reproduce
Servant

FIFTEEN:
Grace
Freedom, Rest Lev 23:6-7

SIXTEEN:
16 Names for Jehovah
16 Attributes of Love 1 Co. 13
Not under law, free Acts 27:34,
37-38

SEVENTEEN:
17 things that cannot separate us
from Gods Love Romans 8
17 differences between Old and
New Covenant Hebrews 12
Spiritual Order
Incomplete, Immature Genesis
37:2

EIGHTEEN:
Bondage, Captivity
Judgement, Destruction Judges
10:7,8 Woman healed after 18
years

NINETEEN:
Faith- 19 people in Faith
Chapter of
Hebrews
Repentance

Ashamed
Barren of Flesh or Spirit

TWENTY:
Redemption
Time of Waiting

Age of going to battle/ war
Jacob waited 20 years for his wives and possessions

TWENTY TWO:
Light
22 Bowls of Oil on the Candle stick
22 sections of Light in Psalms 119

TWENTY FOUR:
Priesthood
Government Rev 4:4-10
24 Elders around the Throne
24 Thrones around the Throne of God

THIRTY:
Launching forth in Ministry
Luke 3:23 Maturity
Redemption price- 30 pieces of silver 30 days in a month

THIRTY THREE:
Jesus went to the cross at 33/ Promise
Jesus rose from the dead at 33/ Resurrection

FORTY:
Probation
Trials, testing Matt 4:2
Temptation
Judgement
Jonah preached judgement to Ninevah for 40 years
Rained 40 days and nights during the flood

FIFTY:
Pentecost

Holy Spirit given 50 days after Jesus' Resurrection

50 years is Jubilee Lev 23:16; 25:10-11 Liberty

SEVENTY:

Restoration
Transference of God's Spirit
Numbers 11:16-29
70 elders

ONE HUNDRED:
Fullness
People of Promise Mark 5:20
Era- 100 years

ONE HUNDRED TWENTY:
Complete Dispensation Of Time
Start of Life in The Spirit
End of Flesh Life Gen 6:3 Eccl 12:7 120 waited in Upper Room Acts 1:5 Power, Demonstration of Holy Spirit Acts 1:15

ONE HUNDRED FORTY FOUR:

God's Redemption Rev 21:17
12x12 God's Perfect Government

THREE HUNDRED:
God's Chosen Judges 7 & 8
Remnant
Gideon's 300 Mighty Men

SIX HUNDRED:
600 Hundred Chariots pursued Israel
Goliath's Spear weighed 600 shekels
Danites sent 600 men to defeat Josiah

SIX HUNDRED SIXTY SIX:

Number of satan- the beast
Bondage
Mark of the beast Rev 13:18

ONE THOUSAND:

Maturity Joshua 3:3-4
Millennial Reign for 1000 years
Fullness of Time

TWO THOUSAND:

Church age ends in Resurrection Joshua 3:4

ONE HUNDRED FORTY FOUR THOUSAND:
Saved Humanity Rev 7:4

COLORS:

BLACK:
Opposite of white, purity Death, Famine Judgement Rev. 6:12
Sin, Ignorance

BROWN:
Flesh
Carnality
Peter 1:24
Barren

BLUE:
Holy Spirit Exodus 35:23
Revelation
Authority
Heaven

Heavenly Visitation
Cleansing

GOLD:
Metal

Holiness Rev 3:18
Holy Spirit Num 8:4
GOD
Kingship

Glory

GRAY:

Mixture Hosea 7:9
Compromise
Deception- Half Truths
Complacency
Dignity, Honor, Age

GREEN:
The Cherubim often manifest as emerald
green lights
Growth, Fruitful

Prosperity, Abundance

ORANGE:
Glory (Amber)

The Cherubim sometimes are seen as amber Danger, Caution,

Blueprint for Hearing GOD

Warning

PINK:
Flesh, Carnal
New Life

PURPLE:
Royalty, Majesty
Kingly, Prince
Authority

Wealth, Rich

RED:
Blood of Jesus Rev. 6:7
Atonement

Forgiveness
Covering, Cleansing
Covenant
Suffering, Sacrifice
Love

Passion, Strong Emotion
Forgiveness
Zealousness
Warfare

Chariots of Fire

SILVER:

Medals
Redemption Price

WHITE:
Purity

Righteousness

Washed Clean by the Blood
Robes of the Redeemed 7 colors combined
Victory

YELLOW:
Sin Psalms 68:13
Infirmity Lev 13:30
Something good, honor

Fear

VEHICLES, TRANSPORTATION:

AIRPLANE:
Ministry flowing in the heavenly realm Ministry on the move

Ministry flying too high or too low

BICYCLE:
Young or Immature Ministry
Ministry flowing in the Holy Spirit

Able to maneuver and go where others can't Motorized or not: Powered by Spirit, or by man

BLIMP:
Heavy and awkward Ministry
Filled with Pride, Puffed up
Moved by any Wind of Doctrine
Weak, Slow to Move or act

BUS:
Sizable Ministry
Group Ministry

SCHOOL BUS: Youth Ministry

CHURCH: Ministry on the move within the Church

TOUR BUS: Christian sightseers, not committed, Carnal

BOAT, SHIP: Local Church Ministry

SAIL BOAT: Ministry Totally Relying upon the Holy Spirit

ROW BOAT: Ministry doing the works of men, flesh

CRUIS SHIP: Ministry that entices by Entertainment

SLAVE SHIP: Ministry that holds people captive or in bondage

HOSPITAL SHIP: Ministry of Healing

WAR SHIP: Influential International Ministry

BATTLE SHIP: Warfare on a larger scale

FISHING BOAT: Ministry of Evangelism, Discipleship

BARGE: Ministry full of Sin, Compromise, Over Burdened and Pride

SUBMARINE : One's hidden agendas, Being under situations and circumstances

Paddle Boat: Ministry of the Flesh, Works, No Spirit Leading

CARGO SHIP: Ministry in the Marketplace, or overburdened

CAR: Personal Ministry, Ministry, Church

CONVERTIBLE CAR: Revelation-based or marketplace Ministry

OLD CAR: Old Ministry, Ministry still operating in the past

NEW CAR: New Ministry, Ministry operating in the Holy Spirit

4 WHEELER: Ground Breaking Ministry

CAR WRECK: Confrontation between GROUPS; Strife between

CAR TIRES: Flat: Ministry operating without the Spirit

LOCATIONS:

ESCALATOR, ELEVATOR:

People, Ministries going in the

Blueprint for Hearing GOD

Spirit:

AIRPORT:
Place of Preparation
Waiting, Change

Ready to soar in the Spirit
Training for prophets, seers

BANK:

Treasure placed in heaven
Protected, safe, secure Storage

BARN:

Place of provision
Church
Storage

BEAUTY SHOP:
Preparation
Vanity
Pride

CAFETERIA:
Church service
Systematic serving of the Word
Picking what you want to eat

Repetitive Ministry
Compromise

CHURCH:
Church service
The Building
The Corporate Structure
Congregation

CITY:

The Church Corporate

CLASSROOM, SCHOOL:
Place of teaching
Instruction

Small groups
Teaching Ministry
Mentoring Ministry
Discipleship

COURTHOUSE, COURTROOM:
Time of Trial, Difficulty
Persecution
Slander, Accusations
Judgement

ELECTRONICS STORE:

Place to acquire heavenly gifts of hearing and seeing

New Level of Communications coming to you

FACTORY:
Place of spiritual productivity
Place of unorganized and inefficient activity

HOSPITAL:

Church with Healing Ministry
Wounded Church that needs healing Place of caring and love, and rest

HOTEL, MOTEL:
Churches together within a City
Place of rest, Communion
Temporary Situation
Transition
Staying temporary at the church

HOUSE:
The Church
Your House
Your Body
Your Family

Home Church

BASEMENT:
Storage area, Memories
Past Experiences
Hidden sins
Carnal nature, lust
Sins of Forefathers, Iniquities hidden

GROUND LEVEL:
Of the Flesh

UPPER LEVEL:
Of the Spirit

ATTIC:
Of the Spirit
Spirit Realm

Stored Memories
Thoughts, Attitudes
Learning, Training

BEDROOM:
Rest, Privacy
Intimacy

Covenant, Union
Dream and Vision Ministry
Teaching/instruction given while sleeping
Resting in God
Transition
Slumber, Laziness

BATHROOM:
Deliverance Ministry
Cleansing, Purging
Healing

Repentance
Confession of Sin

DEN, FAMILY ROOM:
Relaxed Fellowship
Small Groups Ministry

DINING ROOM:
Communion
Table of The Lord
Feasting upon the Word

Fellowship with Brethren
Teaching and Preaching to people

GARAGE:
Storage, Protection

Outreach Ministry

KITCHEN:
Training, Equipping
Mentoring

Teaching Ministry
The Heart
Spiritual Hunger

www.ingramcontent.com/pod-product-compliance
Lightning Source LLC
LaVergne TN
LVHW041544070426
835507LV00011B/920